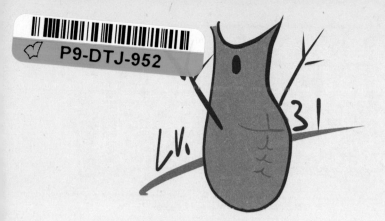

Hirofumi Neda

Has it really been two years already? I doubt I'll ever have such a good time with so many loyal readers again! It's made me so happy. I'll keep supporting *My Hero Academia* publicly and privately going forward, so if you happen to spot me out in the wide world, give me a friendly nod, please. (*bow*)

Anyway, that's all!! Here's hoping we'll meet again somewhere, someday!!

HIROFUMI NEDA began his professional career as a manga artist in 2007, winning the Akatsuka Prize Honorable Mention for his short story "Mom Is a Spy." After publishing several other short stories, he began working as an art assistant to Kohei Horikoshi on *Oumagadoki Zoo* and later on *My Hero Academia*.

KOHEI HORIKOSHI was born in Aichi, Japan, in 1986. He received a Tezuka Award Honorable Mention in 2006, and after publishing several short stories in *Akamaru Jump*, his first serialized work in *Weekly Shonen Jump* was *Oumagadoki Zoo* in 2010. *My Hero Academia* is his third series in *Weekly Shonen Jump*.

VOLUME 5
SHONEN JUMP Manga Edition

STORY & ART BY HIROFUMI NEDA
ORIGINAL CONCEPT BY KOHEI HORIKOSHI

Translation/Caleb Cook
Touch-Up Art & Lettering/John Hunt
Designer/Julian [JR] Robinson
Editor/Hope Donovan

BOKU NO HERO ACADEMIA SMASH!!
© 2015 by Kohei Horikoshi, Hirofumi Neda
All rights reserved.
First published in Japan in 2015 by SHUEISHA Inc., Tokyo.
English translation rights arranged by SHUEISHA Inc.

The stories, characters and incidents mentioned in this publication
are entirely fictional.

No portion of this book may be reproduced or transmitted in any
form or by any means without written permission from the copy-
right holders.

Printed in the U.S.A.

Published by VIZ Media, LLC
P.O. Box 77010
San Francisco, CA 94107

10 9 8 7 6 5 4 3 2 1
First printing, August 2020

viz.com

shonenjump.com

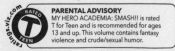

PARENTAL ADVISORY
MY HERO ACADEMIA: SMASH!! is rated
T for Teen and is recommended for ages
13 and up. This volume contains fantasy
violence and crude/sexual humor.

5

STORY & ART BY
HIROFUMI NEDA
ORIGINAL CONCEPT BY KOHEI HORIKOSHI

ALL MIGHT

The top hero whose very name rocks the world. He's also an incompetent newbie teacher.

IZUKU MIDORIYA

A hero fanboy who got his Quirk from All Might.

OCHACO URARAKA

Salt of the earth, woman of the people, and a charming little scamp.

SHOTO TODOROKI

A troubled elite. Ridiculously good-looking.

KATSUKI BAKUGO

A child of the times whose dial is permanently set to "furious."

MOMO YAOYOROZU

TSUYU ASUI

MINORU MINETA

TENYA IDA

FUMIKAGE TOKOYAMI

KYOKA JIRO

HANTA SERO

EIJIRO KIRISHIMA

MINA ASHIDO

DENKI KAMINARI

RIKIDO SATO

STORY

Izuku Midoriya has always idolized heroes—the people who use their Quirk powers to kick evil butt. A chance encounter with All Might gives him the Quirk he needs to attend U.A. High—an elite educational institution for heroes in training! Now there's never a dull moment at U.A.!!

SHOTA AIZAWA

ENDEAVOR

TOMURA SHIGARAKI

KUROGIRI

HIMIKO TOGA

DABI

MY HERO ACADEMIA SMASH!! 5

CONTENTS

DEAR, SWEET DABI

QUEEN MAGNE!!

CALL ME MAGNE.

I LIVE MY LIFE FREE, NOT TIED DOWN BY ANYTHING.

FWP

BLUSH

OOH. ♡

...

?

HUH? WHAT'D YOU SAY...?

OH MY!! AND THAT VOICE—SO SULTRY!!

TREMBLE

TH-THAT THOUSAND-YARD STARE... IT FEELS LIKE YOU'RE LICKING ME ALL OVER WITH YOUR EYES...

BADUM BADUM

W-WHOA, WHAT'S GOING ON?! CUT IT OUT! LEAVE ME ALONE!

GLOMP

FINE, BUT YOU'RE THE ONLY ONE I'LL LET TIE ME DOWN.

THIS IS THE GUY STAIN CHOSE...? GO AHEAD, BUDDY. MAKE GOOD USE OF ME.

SLOWLY BUT SURELY, THE LEAGUE OF VILLAINS GROWS IN POWER...

GRIN

NO. 77!!

LEAGUE OF VILLAINS INITIATES CONFERENCE

SHIGA-RAKI!!

WE'RE REALLY SCRAPING THE BOTTOM OF THE BARREL HERE...

TAP TAP

TAP TAP

TODAY, THREE NEW INITIATES HAVE COME TO ATTEND A SKILLS, DEVELOPMENT AND TEAM-BUILDING CONFERENCE.

(ANTI-) DENTAL PLAN

MOONFISH

HIS TEETH STRETCH. WHAT'S WRONG WITH THIS DUDE?

...

SHAKA

SHAKA

SHAKA

FLESH... MEAT... *HUFF HUFF.*

I LOVE MEAT ALL CHOPPED UP...

I ADMIT, IT MAY BE DIFFICULT TO WORK ALONGSIDE THIS FELLOW.

FRK *SKCH* *SKCH*

WHAT? NO WAY!

SO GO OPEN A BUTCHER SHOP? WARP THIS WACKO AWAY, KUROGIRI.

THAT'S RICH, COMING FROM YOU.

UM...

OKAY, WHAT'RE WE SUPPOSED TO FIND APPEALING ABOUT YOU?

STATE YOUR CASE.

I ACTUALLY PREFER HENCHMEN *WITH* CAVITIES.

I-I'LL GO HEAVY ON THE SUGAR, THEN?

I NEVER GET CAVITIES ...?

RE-JECTED.

ORIGINAL CONTENT

SPINNER

FOLLOWER OF STAIN

GRP

I LIVE ACCORDING TO HIS WILL!

I'M HERE TO MAKE STAIN'S DREAMS A REALITY.

SH-SHIGA-RAKI!!

THIS AIN'T COS-PLAY!!

GET OUT. I'M SICK OF STAIN COSPLAYERS.

HE WANTS TO PURGE SOCIETY OF IDIOTIC BAND-WAGONERS WITH NO REAL CONVIC-TIONS.

STAIN ACTUALLY HATES PUNKS LIKE YOU.

IF YOU REALLY BELIEVED IN THAT, YOU'D CREATE AN ORIGINAL COSTUME.

GET OUT!!

??? I DON'T GET IT...

BUT...DOESN'T INHERITING STAIN'S CONVICTIONS COUNT AS A CONVICTION OF ITS OWN?

FRET

FRUITFUL EXERCISE

NISHI-NIPPORI.

YAYYY!

LET'S PLAY THE GAME WHERE WE GO AROUND NAMING STOPS ON THE YAMANOTE TRAIN LINE. YOU GO FIRST, DABI.

WAIT!

HUH...? OKAY, HOW ABOUT FRUITS?

SHIGARAKI... GOOD ON YOU, THINKING LIKE A LEADER.

WHAT'S THE POINT IN NAMING RAILWAY STATIONS? COME UP WITH A BETTER CATEGORY. GET CREATIVE.

FWIP

AN APPLE A DAY WON'T KEEP ME FROM *KILLING* YOU.

STUPID... WHY DON'T *YOU* THINK OF SOMETHING, THEN?!

HMPH. HEY, SPINNER. HERE'S A CHANCE FOR YOU TO REDEEM YOURSELF. PICK A TOPIC.

I SAY GET CREATIVE, AND YOU COME BACK WITH "FRUITS"? DID YOU GET DROPPED ON YOUR HEAD AS A KID?

GRR

PAY ATTENTION!! AND GO BACK TO KINDER-GARTEN!!

UHH... BANANA?

DABI THE PURE

UGH, OPEN A WINDOW. IT'S STUFFY IN HERE WITH ALL THIS BODY HEAT.

EVERYONE SEEMS TO BE ENJOYING THEM-SELVES.

CANDY... CANDY...

WE LIKE TO PLAY GAMES TO GET TO KNOW NEW MEMBERS BETTER.

OOH, SOUNDS FUN.

HOW ABOUT A GAME?

HMM?

GRAH

THIS AIN'T THE LEAGUE OF BEST BUDDIES !!

NO!! THERE'S NO TIME TO WASTE ON SILLY GAMES!

WHAT NOW?! YOU'VE BEEN ACTING STRANGE ALL DAY! ARE YOU DRUNK?

WHO KNEW DABI WAS SO INNOCENT ...?

TEE HEE

HE'S SUCH A *HARD-LINER*. BUT... I DON'T MIND THAT. ♡

PSST

PSST

9

HANGRY LEADER

HUH...?

JOLT

SORRY.

NO, TOGA. YOU MUSTN'T POINT AT YOURSELF.

WELCOME BACK, TOMURA SHIGARAKI...

CHAK

HMM?

HMPH. WHO EVER HEARD OF A GANG THAT HATES ITS OWN LEADER?

I SAID I WAS HUNGRY, DIDN'T I?

TA—DA

YAKISOBA

DID YOU... ONLY GET ENOUGH FOOD FOR YOUR-SELF?!

I KNEW HE'D DO THAT. THAT'S WHY I HATE HIM THE MOST.

YOU'RE FIRED, DABI.

BUT... NORMALLY ONE PURCHASES ENOUGH FOR EVERYONE!

LIKE I CARE? DON'T PUSH YOUR NORMS ON ME.

GOTTA HAND IT TO HIM

HOW ABOUT THE FIRST IMPRESSIONS GAME?

WUZZAT?

ENOUGH OF THIS IDIOCY. PICK A NEW GAME, KUROGIRI.

THE PERSON POINTED AT THE MOST LOSES.

OH. I LIKE THAT.

WHO HERE SEEMS KINDEST?

ONE PERSON PICKS A QUALITY, AND WE ALL POINT TO WHOEVER EXEMPLIFIES THAT QUALITY.

OKAY, WHO HERE DO WE HATE THE MOST? ONE, TWO... GO!

HUH?

SO LEADER-LIKE!!

ANOTHER BRILLIANT EXECUTIVE DECISION, SHIGARAKI!

AND SINCE I'M HUNGRY, THE LOSER HAS TO GO BUY FOOD.

CAN'T MAKE ME... CAN'T MAKE ME...

FWIP

YOU'RE EXCUSED, TOOTHY.

SHIGARAKI... WE'RE SUPPOSED TO BE MAKING FRIENDS.

AHEM. NOT EVERYONE'S POINTING.

KILLING WITH KINDNESS

SERIOUSLY? I'M THE ONE WHO DID ALL THE WORK.

WHAT AN EXHAUSTING DAY THIS WAS.

MY VALUES PROVED LESS THAN HELPFUL.

I-I REALLY MUST APOLOGIZE.

...BUT NOW I SEE I WAS FOISTING MY OUTDATED VIEWS ON YOU. I WILL REFLECT ON THIS LESSON.

ALL THIS TIME, I'VE LECTURED YOU...

WHAT? DON'T BE DUMB.

G W M P

BUT THAT'S A ONE-PLAYER CAMPAIGN...

HEY. LET'S PLAY THIS VIDEO GAME.

YEAH, YOU GET TO SIT THERE AND WATCH. IT'LL CALM YOU DOWN.

SIGH...

GENERATION GAP

THERE. SEE? GET WITH THE TIMES, GRANDPA.

I'M ON TOMURA'S SIDE. IF YOU WANTED FOOD, YOU SHOULD'VE ASKED.

WHAT?!

G-GRANDPA...?

THAT'S WHAT IT MEANS TO BE COMRADES IN ARMS.

THAT'S RIGHT.

?

I WOULD'VE BOUGHT SOME FOR EVERYONE.

SALUTE

GLIMPSE

I'M SURE YOU'D ALL BE PLEASED IF WE CAME BACK WITH FOOD FOR YOU, YES?

BEHOLD... YOUR HATED NORMS.

HUH?!

NAW, CUZ I'D WANT TO CHOOSE MY FOOD FOR MYSELF.

MEAT... FLESH...

NAH, THAT'D PISS ME OFF. I HATE OWING PEOPLE.

GIVE IT UP, KUROGIRI. DIFFERENT STROKES, AND ALL.

ROCK AND A HARD PLACE

Y'THINK?

HMPH

WHAT AN AMUSING EXERCISE.

WE CAN FINALLY PROVE WHICH IS SUPERIOR— CLASS A OR B?

WERE YOU BOYS EVEN LISTENING? YOU'RE SUPPOSED TO COOPERATE THIS TIME AROUND! NOW GO AHEAD AND DRAW!!

GRRR

GRIN GRIN

LOTS

HUH?! YOU'RE NOT FIT TO LICK MY BOOTS.

ZABAM

TEAM A

THAT'S MY LINE. YOU'D BETTER NOT SLOW ME DOWN!

GAH!! WHY'RE YOU ON MY TEAM?!

THIS CAN'T END WELL...

AS IF, MORON!!

YAP YAP

NO. 78!!

HEROES OFTEN FIND THEMSELVES HAVING TO TEAM UP WITH WHOEVER'S AVAILABLE ON THE SCENE.

MISSION: IN TEAMS OF THREE CHOSEN BY DRAWING LOTS, RESCUE THE CIVILIANS FROM THE COLLAPSED BUILDINGS!!

TODAY'S RESCUE TRAINING WILL THROW CLASSES A AND B INTO THE BLENDER TOGETHER!!

AN A/B SMOOTHIE ...?

UNIVERSAL USER'S GUIDE

WE'RE SCREWED...

LEAP

Kacchan Instruction Manual

HANG ON...

KRAK

YOU GOTTA BE JOKING, RIGHT?!

DURR, WHAT DO I DO HERE, AGAIN?

SHOULD I TEST THOSE HABITS OF HIS?

KACCHAN TIP #1: IF YOU DAWDLE, HE'LL STEP IN TO GET THE JOB DONE.

OOH, NOW IT'S MY TIME TO SHINE.

ZOOM

BAM

IF YOU'RE NOT GONNA HELP, THEN GET OUTTA THE WAY!!

HUHH?!

HUH?

IT WORKED?

SHAKA

SHAKA

BEHOLD! I'M ACCOMPLISHING WHAT EVEN CLASS A'S BEST CANNOT!!

THEY SCORED HIGHER THAN ANY OTHER TEAM.

AS IF!! I'M DOING IT BETTER AND FASTER!!

GROUP PROJECT DYNAMICS

NEITO MONOMA

CLASS B'S PROBLEM CHILD. HE CAN COPY OTHER QUIRKS WITH HIS QUIRK!!

AH HA HA HA!

HMPH. YOUR QUIRK IS EXPLOSION? NICE AND STRONG, BUT HARDLY HELPFUL FOR THIS EXERCISE.

I'LL SHOW YOU!!

BOM

FREEZE

B-BUT...

We're supposed to cooperate.

DASH

Knew it.

Tell someone who cares!

WHATEVER! DO YOUR OWN THING! C'MON, HALF 'N' HALF!

YOU'RE FOLLOWING US ANYWAY, SO DO YOU MIND HELPING?

Ice! Now!

Pick up that end.

YOU UTTER FOOL. I WOULD NEVER ASSIST CLASS A.

WHY DOES HE LOOK SO ECSTATIC?

GLOOMP

GLOOMP

13

NO MOTHER TERESA

I'LL CLEAR THE RUBBLE WHILE YOU LIGHT THE WAY, KAMINARI.

BAM

SURE THING.

UNDER-STOOD.

YOU HANDLE THE RESCUES, SHIOZAKI.

NOW!! DO IT, SHIOZAKI!

NICE! WE MAKE A KILLER TEAM!

INDEED!

THERE'S N-NOTHING WRONG WITH GETTING ENTHUSI-ASTIC.

GASP

W-WAIT, NO!! TAKING PLEA-SURE IN SAVING LIVES IS HIGHLY IMMORAL!!

I MUST BE *PUNISHED* FOR MY SINS!!

THIS GIRL'S INTENSE...

RM RM RM RM RM RM

NO... AND EARLIER, MY EGO LED TO THE DEATH OF THE OLDER GENTLE-MAN...

TURN THE OTHER CHEEK

IBARA SHIOZAKI

THE KINDEST GIRL YOU'LL MEET, BUT OBSESSIVE IN SOME WAYS!!

BOW

GOOD TO BE WORKING WITH YOU, SHIOZAKI.

AGREED. THAT'S WHY WE'LL TRY TO SAVE EVERYONE!

Oh, Lord...

IT PAINS MY HEART TO IMAGINE ASSIGNING A PRIORITY ORDER TO THOSE IN NEED OF SALVATION.

MAMA... WHERE'D YOU GO? IT'S SO COLD...

HEY, SWEET CHEEKS. LEMME GET A HANDFUL OF BOOTY BEFORE I KICK THE BUCKET...

MM-HMM.

HER PRIORITY ORDER'S PRETTY CLEAR.

ZOOM

FEAR NOT. I'LL WARM YOU UP, LITTLE ONE.

MAMA?

14

1-A'S HONORARY TURD

YEAH. WHY?

GRP

JUZO HONENUKI

QUIRK: SOFTENING

HE CAN MAKE STUFF SOFT BY TOUCHING IT.

CAN YOU ADJUST HOW SOFT YOU MAKE STUFF?

LADIES' CLOTHING

OVER HERE, HONENUKI!!

TMP

...AND HER BOTTOM LIKE MARSHMALLOWS!!

ZO

OM!!

MAKE HER RACK AS SOFT AS FRESH-BAKED BREAD...

I CAN'T BELIEVE YOU!!

SPLORT

SPLORT

SO IT'S IN YOUR INTEREST TO GIMME WHAT I WANT.

YOU'RE TRYING TO EARN MY TRUST, RIGHT?

TCH... AND PEOPLE SAY MY FACE IS CREEPY.

HUR HUR HUR HUR HUR

THAT SHOULD WORK.

SPARE ME, OH GREAT HONENUKI!

I'M GETTING THE GIST OF HOW TO HANDLE THIS GUY!

SPLASH SPLASH

WAIT! ARGH! SORRY, SORRY!

IF YOU USE MAX SOFTNESS SETTING ON *HIM*, WILL HE FLUSH?

MASOCHIST MINETA

FIRST, I'LL OBSERVE HOW THEY WORK TOGETHER. THEN, I CAN JOIN IN...

HI THERE.

A DUDE? LAME.

WE'LL NEED TO COOPERATE ON THE FLY, RIGHT?

HANDS OFF!! WHO SAID YOU COULD TOUCH ME?!

GRAB

I GET IT. PUSHING THIS GUY'S BODY TO THE LIMIT MUST UNLOCK THE LATENT POTENTIAL OF HIS QUIRK OR SOMETHING!

S-SORRY.

I SEE. HE NEEDS A RELATIONSHIP BUILT ON TRUST...?

RIBBIT?

I ONLY TAKE THAT KINDA ABUSE FROM *CERTAIN* PEOPLE!!

GRRR

LEADING BY NON-EXAMPLE

...WE PROS WILL BE SHOWING OFF OUR OWN TEAMWORK!!

TO CONCLUDE THIS LESSON...

OOH, I CAN'T WAIT!

OKIE-DOKIE!! ROGER THAT!!

I'LL CHECK AROUND FOR SAFE AREAS. WHEN I GIVE THE SIGNAL, YOU RESCUE PEOPLE FROM THOSE SPOTS.

THIS FOOL, I SWEAR...

NEVER MIND! IT SEEMED SAFE, SO I WENT AHEAD AND SAVED EVERYONE ANYWAY!!

...BUT THE KIDS STILL GOT A KICK OUT OF IT.

Just like I keep saying, All Might's the greatest...

THE TEACHERS' TEAM DIDN'T PROVIDE MUCH OF AN EXAMPLE...

SENPAI NOTICED ME

STARE

ITSUKA KENDO

QUICK TO WHIP OUT THE CHOPS AND SMACKS!! BUT SHE'S ALWAYS IN HIGH DEMAND!!

HEY! USE YOUR AIR BARRIERS AS STRETCHERS FOR THE WOUNDED!

SMAK

SO UNDAUNTED... SO VERY COMPETENT...

I'M SO ENVIOUS OF YOU, KENDO.

Too slow!

WHAP

I TOLDJA TO SET UP TRIAGE, SO GET TO WORK!

OW.

WHAP

YOU TOO! WHY'RE YOU SPACING OUT OVER HERE?

EARTH TO YAOYO-ROZU?!

Y-YES, MA'AM.

BADUM

16

LOW BAR

TOTES APPRECIATE THE LAP PILLOW, TSUYU!

YUP. NOTHIN' TO DO.

SUNDAY

I'M IN HIGH SPIRITS, YES SIREE!!

IT'S DEKU!

DOOO.

DOO DO DO DOO.

TMP TMP

I WISH I COULD GET BOYS EXCITED!

I'M INTRIGUED TOO.

STARE

I WONDER WHAT'S GOT HIM SO EXCITED?

KABI

YOU REALLY THINK THAT LITTLE OF HIM, OCHACO?

WOOOOO!

ROPE

OPAQUE

HOW ABOUT WE FOLLOW HIM IN SECRET?

UMM, BUT WHAT IF HE ENDS UP AT A SKEEVY UNDERGROUND IDOL PERFORMANCE? YIKES...

I-IT'S JUST A POSSIBILITY!

NO. 79!!

IZUKU MIDORIYA (AGE 15). INFAMOUS HERO FANBOY.

WHAT DOES THIS STRANGE CREATURE DO DURING HIS FREE TIME?! THE WORLD NEEDS TO KNOW!!

THE ADVENTURES OF MIDORIYA: DEKU'S DAY OFF

17

TO PERV OR NOT TO PERV

NAKANO BROADWAY

RESEARCH TELLS ME THIS IS THE HOLY LAND OF SORTA SUBCULTURE HERO SHOPS.

GAB GAB

NAKANO BROADWAY, HUH?

OOH.

THIS COUNTS AS "SORTA" SUBCULTURE?!

DON'T YOU WANT TO SMELL ME?

HERO SMELLS SHOP

ALL MIGHT'S SCENT, REPRODUCED!

A FRAGRANCE SHOP?

BAM!!

HE WALKED PAST.

SO HE'S NOT THAT BIG A WEIRDO, AT LEAST.

PHEW

TMP

PLEASE, GOD! STRIKE HIM DOWN BEFORE HE ENTERS THAT SHOP!

OH NO, WHAT IF HE GETS THAT LOOK IN HIS EYES ABOUT THE SMELL-O-RAMA?!

GLANCE GLANCE GLANCE

TIZZY

BAM

WE SHOULD'VE JUST ASKED HIM IF WE COULD COME ALONG!

W-W-WE REALLY SHOULDN'T BE DOING THIS, RIGHT?!

TRUE.

HOW'RE WE GONNA EXPLAIN WHY WE'VE BEEN TAILING HIM?!

HOLD IT, FROGGO!!

I'LL GO ASK HIM.

YANK

OCHACO, HER EYEBALLS!!

YOINK YOINK

HUH? OOPS!!

THERE'S GOTTA BE A MORE TIMELY MOMENT FOR US TO POP OUTTA THE SHADOWS! WE'LL BIDE OUR TIME AND STRIKE!

MAH ONGUE OESN'T OME OUT IKE AT!

18

GEEK DEFENDER

WAIT, OCHACO.

NOT ON MY WATCH.

OH NO, A SHAKE-DOWN!

YO, GIMME YER CASH.

LOOK, IT'S MIDORIYA.

THAT'S A LOTTA THROAT-CLEAR-ING...

KOFF.

AHEM.

KOFF.

KOFF.

HE SWITCHED PLACES WITH THE VICTIM?!

TCH? WHADDYA WANT?!

SHWIP

I'VE ONLY GOT POINTS CARDS...

YOU GOT A CARD? LET'S TAKE A TRIP TO THE ATM.

SORRY, BUT I ONLY HAVE 200 YEN ON ME...

THEY DIDN'T NOTICE THE SWAP!

*ABOUT $2

19

MARKET FORCE

HMM

HERO ⑱

LET'S HAVE A LITTLE FAITH IN HIM, SHALL WE?

PLEASE DON'T LET HIM BUY ONE OF THE PERVY ONES!!

OH, LORD!

SO HE CAME TO BUY A FIGURE?

OPAQUE

HE'S REACHING FOR THE PANTIES-OUT SAILOR UNIFORM MT. LADY!!

RIBBIT RIBBIT

NOOO, NOT THAT ONE!!

¥7,800 -

*ABOUT $78

STILL, IT'S TROUBLING THAT HE KNOWS HOW IT SHOULD BE PRICED.

LOOKS LIKE HE'S NOT BUYING IT.

So sincere...

HER

EXCUSE ME, SIR, BUT YOU HAVE THIS PRICED AT DOUBLE THE GOING RATE.

NO ONE'S PERFECT, GIRL.

AWW, DEKU...

SHWIP

SHWIP

DAMN! THE INTERNET SAID THIS SPOT WAS PERFECT FOR SHAKING DOWN NERDS.

GAHH!

WHAT THE HELL! WE'RE COMING UP EMPTY-HANDED EVERY DAMN TIME.

LOOKS LIKE...

...BEING A MEAT SHIELD FOR THESE 'OTHER' DWEEBS!?

SHWIP

...HE'S SPENDING HIS DAY OFF...

SKID

AWW, DEKU...

TWINGE

BADUM

THERE'S NO MONEY HERE! JUST THIS ONE KID WITH SOME SORTA HARDENING QUIRK!

YEAH, LET'S BLOW THIS SPOT AND FIND SOMEWHERE ELSE.

THE HERO WE NEED

HUH? THAT'D DEFEAT THE POINT OF ME HELPING YOU! KEEP IT!

BOW BOW

TH-THANK YOU! HERE, A REWARD!

ARE YOU SURE? THEY WERE KICKING YOUR STOMACH PRETTY HARD BACK THERE.

*ABOUT $200

GET-TING KICKED IS TRAIN-ING?! JUST JOIN A GYM!!

BAM

NO WORRIES! THAT'S GOOD TRAINING FOR ME...

NAW, JUST ANOTHER HERO FANBOY LIKE YOU!

BUT ANYWAY, THOSE GUYS MIGHT RETALIATE...

SNAP

W-WAIT. ARE YOU A HERO?

IF YOU LOCK EYES WITH THEM, DON'T PANIC—JUST WALK STRAIGHT AHEAD!

HE REALLY IS TRYING TO HELP...

IT'S BETTER NOT TO GET DRAGGED IN.

MIXED BAG

HUGGING CARDBOARD? GO HUG A PINCUSHION INSTEAD, YOU!!

WHOA! URARAKA? GIRLS? WAIT, WHY A PINCUSHION?!

COOL IT, YOU TWO.

W-WHY'DJA HAVE TO PICK UP THAT THING?!

GRR GRR

OH? THE SMELLS SHOP?!

WHY'M I HERE, YOU ASK? JUST SHOPPING OVER... THERE...

ACK! I COULDN'T HELP MYSELF!

ACK! NO, I MEAN... UGHH!!

ZERO SMELLS SHOP

TURN

S...

YOU DO?! I DIDN'T WANNA KNOW THAT!!

YOU DUG YOUR OWN GRAVE, GIRL!

What a coincidence!

Wow.

I-I SHOP THERE TOO SOMETIMES!

WEIRDO!!

GAH!

SILENT

DEKU'S STOCK ROSE AND FELL THAT DAY, WITH A SLIGHT NET LOSS.

C'MON, LET'S SHOP!

DON'T BE EMBARRASSED. THERE'S AN ODOR FOR EVERYONE IN THERE...

SILENT

UGH, DEKU?!

THE WORLD'S A SCARY PLACE WHEN YOU DON'T GOT A STRONG QUIRK.

YEAH, THIS WAS A GOOD LESSON.

MIDORIYA REALLY THOUGHT TEN STEPS AHEAD ON THIS ONE.

CAFE Geno

CAFE Geno

AND THAT'S WHY HE'S SO SENSITIVE TO BULLYING?

RIGHT. ALL THAT BAD BLOOD WITH BAKUGO...

MIDORIYA DIDN'T HAVE AN EASY TIME UP THROUGH MIDDLE SCHOOL...

DEKU... YEAH, HE'S DESTINED FOR GREAT-NESS...

FOR SURE!! MAKES ME WANNA ROOT FOR HIM.

MIDORIYA CAN BE AN ODDBALL, BUT I BELIEVE HE'LL MAKE A GREAT HERO.

ME TOO.

RIBBIT

UGH, DEKU ?!

I KNEW THE PROMO WOULD BE ENDING TODAY, SO I JUST [MAD]E THIS [T]OUT WAY.

WOO HOO! JUST AS PLANNED!

SMOOCH SMOOCH

HE'LL BE THE GREATEST OF ALL T—

WHO'S JOKE IS IT ANYWAY?

NONSENSE! HAVING A GO-TO GAG IS A TRICK OF THE TRADE FOR POPULAR PROS!

BAM!!

THAT'S SOME STRONG HAIR!

ISN'T COMEDY SORTA OUTSIDE OF A HERO'S WHEELHOUSE?

I SEE YOUR POINT!! LET US FORMULATE SOME GAGS!

Even you, Ida?

PLENTY OF OTHER HEROES ALSO HAVE HILARIOUS GIMMICKS...

IT'S TRUE. ALL MIGHT SHOWS WHAT HE'S MADE OF WHEN HE GETS BIG LAUGHS EVEN IN DISASTER ZONES.

GET CREATIVE, AND TRIUMPH BY GETTING THE MOST LAUGHS!

BAM

SOME OF THEM LOOK HARD TO PLEASE...

JUDGES

HERE'S YOUR PANEL OF FIVE JUDGES, EACH WITH A PREFERRED STYLE!

WHY'S THIS FEELING MORE AND MORE LIKE A GAME-SHOW?!

BY THE WAY, IF YOU FLOP OUT THERE, THERE'S A TRAP-DOOR!

KA-CH AK!!

SOMETIMES, A HERO'S GOTTA BE THE ONE TO TURN FROWNS UPSIDE DOWN!!

SO, CAN ANYONE GUESS WHAT TODAY'S TRAINING IS?!

NO. 80!!

BZZT, WRONG! IT'S COMEDY TRAINING!!

RESCUE TRAINING?!

COMEDY?! WE'RE GONNA HIT 'EM DIRECTLY IN THE FUNNY BONES?!

GOODBYE, MINETA

That's the (self-styled) god of comedy, Minoru Mineta!

Hope you're all ready to wet yourselves laughing.

BABAM

Move aside, amateurs. A real pro's comin' through!

Awful!!

In so many ways!!

BOOM SHAKA

BOOM SHAKA

I have a ball.

I have a ball.

Truly terrible!!

LEAP

DONG

A man!!

Ahem... you've just been expelled.

PSST PSST

HMM?

JUDGES

MERCY KILLING

I hope you all enjoy!!

The first act is my-self, Tenya Ida!!

SHABAM!!

Full circle man.

WOMP

WOMP

Running man.

...Man!!

OOK.

Ape...

WOMP

WOMP

It was then that they realized the trapdoor wasn't for entertainment value, but to put bad performers out of their misery.

FLOP

KA CHAK

URARAIZAWA

GOING FOR MORE SUBTLE HUMOR, PERHAPS?!

OOH! OUR NEXT CONTESTANT LOOKS SERIOUS!

SHP

AN IMPRESSION!!

BAM

HEY. IN YOUR SEATS, NOW.

MUSS MUSS

HMM? WHY ARE YOU HERE, MIC?

PIPE DOWN, KAMINARI.

I CAN TOTALLY SEE THIS HAPPENING!!

UNLESS THIS IS SOME SORT OF RATIONAL DECEPTION?

MEGA YUKS

ENGLISH ISN'T UNTIL FOURTH PERIOD.

HA HA HA HA HA

A MASTERPIECE! BRAVO!

YUK HA HA

STOP LAUGHING, MIC! THIS HITS TOO CLOSE TO HOME...

YUK HA

ET TU, PRINCIPAL?!

SHE'S SPOT-ON!!

MEGA YUKS

HANDSOME HUMOR

SKETCH (PAD) COMEDY?!

HERE'S A STORY ABOUT A CAT I SAW THIS MORNING.

FWP

I'M STILL NOT SEEING HOW THIS TRAINING IS PRACTICAL.

AND IT'S THE PERFECT THING FOR HIM... THEY'RE SURE TO LOVE IT.

THAT'S AN OPTION, I GUESS! A WAY NOT TO FLOP TOO HARD.

Damn him.

...IT WAS TWO CATS.

BUT WHEN I STARED AT THE BLACK CAT, I REALIZED...

FLIP

BADUM

Me

Me

PRETTY BOY PRIVILEGE!

SOMETHING FEELS UNFAIR HERE.

CHUCKLE CITY

THAT EARNED SOME CHUCKLES! FINALLY, A CONTESTANT PASSED THE TEST!

PHEW.

FEMALE GAZE

HOW ABOUT A BEEFCAKE SHOW, JIRO?

I'm racking my brain...

SHAKA SHAKA

NO WAY, NOT THAT!

UGH, WHAT DO I DO? THIS'S S'POSED TO BE THE HERO COURSE, YEAH?

BAM

SHE'S GOING FOR IT?!

HMM? ARE YOU TWO HUNKS HERE FOR LITTLE OLD ME?

MEGA YUKS

OOOH!

A CHAIR WITH HEATING AND COOLING FUNCTIONS? NICE.

WHAT'M I EVEN SAYING?

A GIRL NEEDS A SEAT. MIND HELPING ME OUT?

PANT PANT

MEGA YUKS

WHAT I WOULDN'T GIVE FOR A SEAT LIKE HERS!!

THAT GIRL'S GOT MOVES...

SHP

DARK HORSE

HOW WOULD THAT AMOUNT TO EFFECTIVE TRAINING, THOUGH?

MAYBE HE CAN RIDE THAT MOMENTUM?

SHOJI'S NEXT. HE'S GOT A TOUGH ACT TO FOLLOW.

BAM

FOR REAL?!

I... I'LL BE TAKING OFF MY MASK.

BAM

SECRET

TUG

FWP

IT'S

OHH!

HM?

GAH!!

HE GOT US GOOD! DANG, ANOTHER BIG WINNER!

YEAHHH!

MEGA YUKS

CAN I GO HOME YET?

CLEVER...

AN UNEXPECTED PRANKSTER.

STRAIGHT MEN

WAIT, LOOKIT BAKUGO THOUGH...

HUH? A COMEDY DUO?! NO FAIR!!

BAM

HEY, ALL!! WE ARE "BAKUGO 'N' ROCK"! THANKS FOR COMING OUT TODAY!!

IS THIS TOO MUCH? MAYBE? GAH HA HA!!!

THE PRINCIPAL IS LETTING IT FLY!!

WISH WE'D KNOWN THAT SOONER!

FWP

I'LL ALLOW IT.

HMM, GIVEN THAT IT'S SUCH A RISKY MOVE FOR BOTH OF THEM...

I CAN TAKE WHATEVER YOU THROW AT ME!!

HARDENING

KRK KRK

BRING IT!! HIT ME WITH YOUR WORST QUIPS AND COMEBACKS, DUDE!!

SILENT

?

NOBODY LAUGHED, BUT THEIR HEARTSTRINGS WERE TUGGED BY THE AWKWARDEST COMEDY DUO ON EARTH.

WE DIDN'T EVEN HAVE TIME TO REHEARSE, YOU DUMMY.

YES, EXACTLY, THAT'S WHAT I'M TALKING ABOUT!! KEEP IT COMING.

YOU GOTTA MAKE A JOKE BEFORE I CAN FIRE BACK, YOU IDIOT.

ANOTHER DIRECT HIT! OOF!

B-O-O-O-M!!!

SWELL GUY, THAT KIRISHIMA FELLA

TINY TITTER

CHAK

THE SERIES' PROTAGONIST

I AM HEEERE-O! GET IT? LIKE "I AM HERE," BUT ALSO "HERO"?

I GUESS YOU'RE NOT GREAT AT LAUGHING OR BEING FUNNY.

SHUT UP!! SO STUPID.

HUH?!

Here I go! GAH HA HA!

HEY, BAKUGO. YOU'RE NOT GONNA GIVE IT A SHOT?

...BUT I SURE CAN LAUGH!!

WHEREAS I MIGHT NOT BE A COMEDY GENIUS...

GRIN

CUZ WHATEVER YOU TRY, I'LL BE SURE TO LAUGH FOR YOU!!

RUNNING FROM A CHALLENGE AIN'T LIKE YOU! GET OUT THERE, DUDE!!

CHARACTER PROFILES!!

ONE LAST ROUND OF

THESE PROFILE PAGES!!

KEEP READING TO

THE VERY END.

PLEASE?

FUMIKAGE TOKOYAMI

THIS BIRD'S ALWAYS SUAVE AND SMOOTH! HE TREATS THE LADIES WITH CARE AND RESPECT, AND LETS HIS SILENCE DO MOST OF THE TALKING... YOU'LL END UP FALLING FOR HIM TOO, NO DOUBT!!

HE'S KIND OF PUTTING ON AIRS, THOUGH, SO SOMETIMES HIS ATTEMPTS TO LOOK COOL FLOP AND HE FINDS HIMSELF IN FREEFALL!!

BUT PEOPLE SAY THAT EVEN THAT SIDE OF HIM IS ENDEARING...

MOBILE GAMES

WOO!! WE DEFEATED THE DEVIL CEO!

HEH HEH. JUST CALL ME THE ZERO MICRO-TRANS-ACTIONS QUEEN.

NICE MOVES, URARAKA!

HRM?

HOW MANY TIMES MUST I REPRIMAND YOU BEFORE THE MESSAGE STICKS? AND EVEN YOU, URARAKA?

THAT INFERNAL GAME AGAIN?! YOU THREE HAVE BEEN GAMING TOO MUCH LATELY!

STOMP

FWEE FWEE FWEE

IT'S GREAT TEAMWORK TRAINING. YOU'D BE SURPRISED.

Yeah. Chill.

IT'S JUST A VIDEO GAME, MAN.

HRM... WOULD I NOW?

NO. 81!!

THIS BOY...

...IS SERIOUS ABOUT EVERY-THING!

THE ADVENTURES OF IDA: A CLASS PRESIDENT'S JOB

SELLING POINT

IT COULD BE GOOD TRAINING, I SUPPOSE, THOUGH I DON'T SEE HOW.

WHAT EXACTLY... IS FUN ABOUT THIS?

HMM

!! BZZZ

OF ALL THE... I WAS JUST ABOUT TO DO SOME EXTRA STUDYING...

Transponder Snail
You gotta fight the good fight with us, Ida Sensei!

Ochamochi
Yeah! Mr. Full-Time Employee!

Sero Hanta
Please and thank you.

BLIP
BLIP
BLIP

W-WE WON!!

ONLY BARELY, BUT THIS SENSE OF ACHIEVEMENT IS LIKE NOTHING ELSE!!

PANT PANT

PANT

30 MIN. LATER

YESSS!!

IT'S NO WONDER THEY'RE ADDICTED TO THIS...

GAH!! I'LL NEED TO FORMULATE A STRATEGY TO RESIST...

HMPH! AND THIS FEELING OF SOLIDAR- ITY!!

Ochamochi
Ur a god

Transponder Snail
Godly

Sero Hanta
God tier

BLIP
BLIP
BLIP

SHAKA

SHAKA

BEAM

ON A LUCKY ROLL

IN THIS GAME, YOU PLAY AS OFFICE WORKERS BEATING UP THEIR MEAN OLD BOSSES.

THIS IS *CORPO- RATE DRONE'S REVENGE!* CDR FOR SHORT!

GO ON. TRY THE GACHA ROLL.

THIS ONE'S BEEN EVERYONE'S FAV FOR YEARS!

THIS IS STILL UNCLEAR TO ME...

ROLL

HRM?

HRM.

FOR REAL? TALK ABOUT BEGIN- NER'S LUCK!!

WHOA!! YOU ROLLED A FULL-TIME EMPLOYEE WITH BENEFITS AT A BROAD- CASTING COMPANY ?!

ULTIMATE RARE

LET'S GET THIS ROLLING!

BA

BA

M

YEAH, A DIRECTOR- LEVEL CHARACTER CAN KILL THE BOSS REAL EASY.

ARGH! YOU ONLY GET THAT KINDA LUCK WHEN YOU'RE *NOT* HOPING FOR IT.

I SEE.

WAS IT GOOD?

WA

HH!

JUNKIE	DAILIES

HE'S A TOTAL ADDICT NOW. SPENDING REAL MONEY AND EVERYTHING.

REALLY?!

UN-FRIENDED YOU? YEAH, US TOO.

HEY, GET THIS... IDA, HE...

SEEMS LIKE IT...

PSST PSST PSST

THE NEXT DAY

TCH!! TODAY'S WEDNESDAY, SO...

THAT MEANS WE GET A BONUS QUEST! I WANNA PLAY SO BAD!

HE'S GOT A BUNCH OF SPARE PHONE CHARGERS.

AND CHECK OUT HIS COSTUME'S BELT.

HE'S IGNORING TRAINING LESSONS IN ORDER TO KEEP PLAYING, EVEN...

MAYBE JUST ONE QUICK ROUND...

FIDGET FIDGET

WE'RE WASTING WAKING HOURS NOT PLAYING THE GAME.

AH!! APOLO-GIES! I'M PAYING ATTENTION!!

FLIK FLIK

BOW

IDA. IF YOU'D RATHER BE ELSE-WHERE, THEN LEAVE.

IDA'S GOING AT IT FULL THROTTLE!!

TAP TAP VAM

HMM...?

...HE'S STILL RUNNING THOSE QUESTS.

DOOM DOOM

E-EVEN AFTER SENSEI SCOLDED HIM...

OOH

Ochacorny

YOU GOTTA BE KIDDING... HE ALREADY OUTRANKS ME?!

BACK

FRIENDS:

ida822
Rank: 325
Last Login: 5 minutes ago

stickytape
Rank: 112
Last Login: 3 hours ago

godkingzeus
Rank: 115
Last Login: 3 hours ago

HUH...?

WE GOTTA GET HELP FROM PEOPLE WHO'D NEVER GET HOOKED IN A MILLION YEARS.

SHAKA SHAKA

W-WHAT NOW? THIS IS GETTING BAD...

LIKE TOKOYAMI AND TODOROKI?

I SUSPECTED HIS SERIOUSNESS WOULD BACKFIRE IN A DANGEROUS WAY SOMEDAY.

...EVERY-THING.

SERIOUS ABOUT...

REALLY?! IT'S THAT BAD?!

EXACTLY.

NO FREAKIN' WAY!! HOW'D THIS HAPPEN?!

DOOM!!

YOU'RE FRIENDS WITH HIM, RIGHT? MAYBE HE'LL LISTEN TO YOU.

WE FEEL KINDA RESPONSIBLE, CUZ WE GOT HIM HOOKED.

T-TRUE ENOUGH!! I'LL GIVE IT A SHOT!!

VERY WELL.

IDA SENSEI, YOU HANDLE THE SENIOR DIRECTOR FOR US.

NICE. I ROLLED A SECRETARY.

I'LL LURE THE BOSS OUT.

TAP TAP TAP TAP TAP TAP TAP.

CDR IS THE BEST.

TAP TAP-TAP TAP TAP TAP

MIDORIYA? YOU TOO?!

OUR NATION IS DOOMED!!

TH-THE FUTURE LOOKS BLEAK...

10 YEARS LATER: MHA: NECKBEARD EDITION

FORGET THAT! YOU GOTTA BREAK FREE!

SHAKA SHAKA

THERE'S AN ALL MIGHT EVENT.

P-PULL IT TOGETHER, MAN!

ESPECIALLY CUZ YOU'RE MOST LIKELY TO GO FULL OTAKU!! NEVER GO FULL OTAKU!!

GRP

A CLASS PRESIDENT'S JOB

...SO I REQUESTED HELP FROM THE OTHERS FOR A BIT OF PERFORMATIVE REVERSE PSYCHOLOGY.

IT WAS CLEAR THAT YOU THREE WERE HEADED DOWN THE DARK PATH OF ADDICTION...

HUHH?!

IT IS THE PRESIDENT'S RESPONSIBILITY TO ENSURE THAT THEIR CLASSMATES LIVE WELL-ROUNDED LIVES.

SO YOU WERE ALL JUST PRETENDING TO BE HOOKED?!

OH, IDAAA!!

PHEW

INDEED!

HOW ABOUT WE ALLOT THIRTY MINUTES EACH DAY FOR YOUR GAMING?

5:30 – 6:00 GAME TIME

RECREATION IS IMPORTANT, BUT EVERYTHING IN MODERATION, NOW!

EH? SHP

I'M HOPING YOU CAN ALL RANK UP WITH TODAY'S DAILY QUEST!!

FWEE FWEE FWEE

ATTENTION ALL!! IT'S GAME TIME!! SHUT OFF THAT TELEVISION!!

WAY TO TAKE THE FUN OUT OF IT...

A GACHA GOTCHA

WE MADE A MISTAKE!!

WAAH

AIZAWA SENSEI!! YOU GOTTA HELP US!!

HA! YOUR USERNAME'S JUST YOUR REAL NAME?

NOT YOU TOO, SENSEI!!

GET OFF MY DESK.

BAM

CAN THIS WAIT?

JUST AS PLANNED!

GLOOM

IT'S ALL OVER IF ONLY WE HADN'T SHOWN IDA THAT STUPID GAME...

HA HA HA. WELL, YOU SEE, I COULD TELL...

...THAT IT WAS TOO FUN FOR CHIDING ALONE TO STOP YOU.

H-HUH? IDA?!

BUT YOU WERE REDUCED TO A TAP-HAPPY GACHA MONKEY?!

BUMPY START

HUH? MORE INTERN-SHIPS?!

YES. YOU TWO DIDN'T EARN ENOUGH CREDITS.

EH?

HUH ?!

THIS IDIOT, SURE, BUT WHY ME?!

TELL ME!

YOU? YOU FAILED OUTRIGHT.

YOUR MENTOR PUT IN A REQUEST FOR EXTRA TRAINING.

AS FOR YOU, MIDORIYA, THE PAPERWORK WAS MISSING, AND YOUR MENTOR WON'T PICK UP THE PHONE.

WHICH MEANS YOU'D GET NO CREDITS AT ALL, AND YOU'D BE HELD BACK A YEAR.

PLEASE, NO!!

HOT SPRING VACATION

UNPRECEDENTED.

THE PRINCIPAL THOUGHT UP A SCHEME TO HELP, MIDORIYA.

NO THANK YOU.

Please?

DIS-MISSED.

YOU'LL BE DOING IT TOGETHER.

NO. 82!!

BAKUGO AND MIDORIYA

REPORT TO THE STAFF ROOM AFTER SCHOOL.

SOME-HOW, THIS IS...

...INTERN-SHIP: REDUX.

KACCHAN, LEASHED

ASSIGNMENT #1: WALKING AN OLD DOG

BAAAN

WHAT IS UNCLEAR, EXACTLY?

WHAT'S THE POINT OF THIS?!

POP

POP

WHAT THE &#$%...

THIS GROUNDBREAKING TRAINING WILL TEACH YOU TO BE AWARE OF YOUR SURROUNDINGS AT ALL TIMES.

SIMPLE ENOUGH!

POIK

CLAP

WHOEVER STEPS OUT OF LINE WILL END UP TUGGING ON HIS OWN ROPE AND LOSING POINTS.

WHY'S IT GOTTA BE *THAT*?!

FOOM

BOM

LET THE DOG LEAD YOU ALONG THE WALK.

IF EITHER OF YOU FALLS TO ZERO POINTS, I'LL UNDO THE SEAMS ON YOUR CLOTHES.

BROWN-NOSER

I AM NO FAN OF THOSE WHO SHIRK THEIR PERSONAL GROOMING.

AN UPTIGHT DUDE WHO PREACHES THE VIRTUES OF EXCELLENCE!!

FWIP

TO BE HONEST, I WASN'T THRILLED ABOUT TAKING ON ANOTHER MENTEE.

NO. 4 HERO: BEST JEANIST

YES, SIR!

EXCITED TO BE IN THE PRESENCE OF NO. 4

BADUM BADUM

SLICK

AND YET, IZUKU MIDORIYA... YOU SEEM TO HAVE TURNED THINGS AROUND?

INGRATIATING ONESELF TO ONE'S AFFILIATED ORGANIZATIONS IS KEY IN OUR QUIRK-BASED SOCIETY.

KABOOM

CUT IT OUT, YOU LITTLE SUCK-UP!!

OW!

"COOPERATION" IS THE CONCEPT I WILL DRILL INTO YOU THIS TIME.

SLICK

SO YOU *MUST* LEARN TO RISE TO EXPECTATIONS.

HE'S GREAT WITH KIDS, PART 2

WHO'S A GOOD BABY?

ARGH!

HUH?!

ASSIGNMENT #2: BABYSITTING

YOU REFUSE TO LEARN YOUR FUNDAMENTALS.

YOU MUST PACIFY THE INFANT.

BOOM!!

WHAT'S THIS GOT TO DO WITH ANYTHING?! GIMME SOME REAL HERO TRAINING!!

WHAT THE?

WAH WAH

GAH!

GRAAH

NO WAY! I NEVER AGREED TO THIS!!

SOME SORT OF SYMPATHETIC PSYCHIC LINK PERHAPS...?

RAWR!

RAWR!

SHAH-AP-OO!

SHUT UP, YOU!!

KACCHAN-GO-ROUND

YOU GONNA MAKE IT, KACCHAN?

SHUT YER TRAP...

5 MINUTES LATER

...

QUIT IT!! YOU'RE NOT S'POSED TO TUG ON PURPOSE!

GWUH

YANK

WHY THIS? WHY WITH HIM?!

DAMN IT!! WHY WHY?!

SO HOW'M I DOWN TO ONE POINT WHILE HE'S STILL GOT NINE?!

I NICKNAMED HIM "DEKU" CUZ HE WAS ALWAYS CLUMSY AND USELESS!

KACCHAN'S FINALLY BROKEN!!

YIKES!

SNAP

ARGH!! SHUT UP, SHUT UP, SHUT UP, BRAIN!!

FOOM

35

TRANSCENDENCE	TABLE MANNERS

WHOZZAT?

IT SEEMS WE'VE FINALLY SUPPRESSED THAT EGO OF HIS.

LUNCH: FEEDING SOMEONE ELSE

...WITHOUT IT, HE'S BASICALLY LEFT WITH NOTHING AT ALL.

EGO

OF COURSE! SINCE KACCHAN'S MIND IS BASICALLY 99 PERCENT EGO...

SO THIS *REALLY* ISN'T GONNA END WELL FOR ME...

GET USED TO IT.

HUH?

UM, YOU SHOULD KNOW, BAKUGO ACTUALLY HATES MY GUTS...

SHAKA SHAKA

HONK

POKE

THE REAL TEST COMES WHEN WE MUST GIVE AID TO THOSE WE DISLIKE... VILLAINS EVEN, SOMETIMES.

PROCEED.

NATURALLY, EVERYONE WOULD SEEK TO SAVE THOSE THEY'RE FOND OF.

RIGHT. ONLY SUPPRESSED. NOT GONE.

S-SORRY.

BOOM BOOM

BOOM BOOM

YOU'RE DEAD MEAT...

I never learn.

OF COURSE THE TALENTED MR. BAKUGO HAD THE SKILLS TO PULL THIS OFF.

NO WAY! HE'S FEEDING ME BETTER THAN I FEED MYSELF!?

SORRY, BUD... I KNOW, THIS SUCKS, BUT C'MON... PLEASE?

HUH?

36

DETACHED RETINAS

CUZ I'LL STILL MATCH YOUR MOVES, 100 PERCENT!!

BAM

WHATEVER, KACCHAN! DO WHAT YOU WANT!!

THERE'S MORE THAN ONE WAY TO "COOPER-ATE."

$#%&@#&$@&$@#!!!

BOOOM

SHADDUP! QUIT TALKIN' LIKE YER BETTER THAN MEEEE!!

POW

OKAY... NOW!!

I'LL DO IT...

...ALL ON MY OWN!!

TO THINK THAT A FRAUGHT FRIENDSHIP COULD GIVE RISE TO SUCH BEAUTIFUL TEAMWORK...

EYES

WE DID IT!

FORCED ME TO PLAY YOUR GAME, DIDJA?!

MEANS TO AN END

THIS MAN'S QUIRK IS *MIRAGE*. HE'S UNTOUCHABLE UNLESS YOU STRIKE BOTH HALVES AT ONCE.

VWOON

FINAL ASSIGNMENT: FALIX VILLAIN BATTLE

COME AT ME, BOYS.

LET'S DO THIS, KACCHAN!!

KACCHAN?!

DASH **DURR**

SHOW ME THE FRUITS OF YOUR TRAINING.

SO IT WAS HIS EGO DRIVING HIM TO HELP OTHERS...?

N-NO LUCK! HE'S GOT NO URGE TO SAVE PEOPLE FROM VILLAINS ANYMORE!

KACCHAN MIGHT BE UNORTHO-DOX, BUT THE HERO WORLD NEEDS HIS TALENTS!

I MEAN, I GUESS THERE ARE HEROES WHO ONLY GET INTO THE BIZ TO BE NUMBER ONE!

37

MISSING PILLARS

MAID CAFE!!

MAID CAFE!!

ARM-WRESTLING!!

MOCHI STAND!!

HAUNTED HOUSE!!

...AND HAVE PEOPLE HANG THEIR WISHES FOR THE REST OF THE YEAR ON THE TANABATA TREE, IN EXCHANGE FOR A CHARITABLE DONATION!!

TANABATA CHARITY

DONATIONS

WE SHOULD FORGO THE ECCENTRIC...

ABSOLUTELY NOT!!

FWP

YEAH. WE NEVER HAVE THIS MUCH TROUBLE...

DOOM

YEAH. THIS ISN'T COMING TOGETHER AT ALL.

SOMETHING'S WEIRD HERE.

3 HOURS LATER

DOOM

MEANWHILE

LEAP

MAID CAFE

IT'S LIKE THE WHOLE MOOD IS DIFFERENT... SOMEHOW.

*SEE PREVIOUS CHAPTER

NO. 83!!

THIS YEAR, U.A. IS HOLDING A TANABATA FESTIVAL.

OKONOMIYAKI

EACH CLASS WILL PREPARE A STALL OR EXHIBIT, AND THE PROCEEDS WILL GO TO CHARITY.

SUMMER FESTIVAL! WOOO! WHEN IS IT?!

*COMPOSITE IMAGE

TOMORROW.

OF COURSE IT IS!!

38

1-A IN DECLINE

WHAT'S THEIR THEME?

OLD-FISH SCOOPING

MOCHI

MAIDS INSIDE

ARM-WRESTLING

SILENT

WE'LL DO ANYTHING FOR YOU!

WELL, I WAS JUST OUT WALKING MONOMA, SO...

C-COULD YOU BE... CUSTOMERS?

WHAT'S THAAAT? FAILING MISERABLY?

SNIFF

SNIFF

YANK

SNIFF

APROPOS OF NOTHING, CLASS B IS RAKING IT IN—URK!

HONESTLY, OUR EXHIBIT IS A BIG FLOP, AND EVERYONE'S KINDA DOWN IN THE DUMPS.

AND WE CAN PAY WITH THE CASH I GET FROM FARMING HIM.

WINK

OHH, GOOD IDEA!!

DON'T WORRY, I'M PREPARED TO RAKE *HIM* IN IF HE MISBEHAVES.

You defeated Neito. You earned 13,650 G.

(BAKUGO + MINETA) ÷ 2

GOOD THING I'M HERE!

AH HA HA HA HA! SALES ARE BOOMING, AND I CAN'T STOP LAUGHING!

CREP

WH

CLASS B

KLANG

LEASH

OH, I KNOW!! HOW ABOUT WE GO SPY ON CLASS A'S STUPID STALL?!

YUP. IF YOU GET OUT OF LINE, I'LL JUST TUG YOU BACK.

THAT'S NO WAY TO TREAT ME...

AH HA HA HA

IS THE LEASH REALLY NECESSARY?

NOOO!! CAN I BE BAKUGO AT LEAST...?

LIKE THIS.

YOU DON'T THINK SO? BASICALLY, WE HAVE TO HANDLE YOU LIKE CLASS A HANDLES MINETA.

SMOOCH

39

MOCHIPALOOZA

CAN I TRY... "AQUATIC PRISONERS TRAPPED IN A MINIATURE CISTERN FOR YOUR AMUSEMENT"?

DOES SHE EVEN KNOW WHAT IT IS?

ONE ORDER OF THE AQUA THING!

Lost handily

SORRY, I WAS REALLY HOPING FOR SOMETHING TO DRINK...

YOU GET THREE SCOOP ATTEMPTS.

Goldfish scooping

...OSHIRUKO...

OH. IT'S...

HOT HOT

NOPE! JUST MY FAVORITE MOCHI-BASED DISHES.

I DON'T SUPPOSE YOU'VE GOT ICED COFFEE?

WHY'S SHE SO PROUD OF THAT?!

HUP!

CURSED MENU

IT'S SO GLOOMY IN HERE. WHAT WENT WRONG?

SILENT

WE HAVE TWO CUSTOMERS.

IT'S A MENU, BUT WHAT'S WHAT, EXACTLY...?

Woman in White Who Fell into a Well...650 yen

Tears from Hades w/Sweat-stained Anguish...350 yen

Aquatic Prisoners Trapped in a Miniature Cistern for Your Amusement...200 yen

Laughing Puppet Tells You a Tale From Beyond the Grave

*ABOUT $2, $6.50 AND $3.50

..."TEARS FROM HADES WITH SWEAT-STAINED ANGUISH."

ERM, I'LL HAVE THE...

WHICH ONE IS A NORMAL DRINK?

REALLY?

AH! GOOD CHOICE.

MOCHI

I ORDERED AN ARM-WRESTLING MATCH...?

BAM

ORDER UP! BUT DON'T EXPECT MERCY JUST CUZ YOU'RE A CHICK!

CHANNELED

URARAKA'S REALLY NAILING THESE IMPRESSIONS.

"GEE, S-SORRY, KACCHAN."

"DEKU!! GET YOUR UGLY MUG OUTTA MY SIGHT!!"

THERE! THAT'S IT!!

GASP

WHAM

"ALSO, WHAT THE HELL'S WITH THIS MENU? NONE OF IT MAKES ANY DAMN SENSE!!"

KEEP IT UP, URARAKA!

S-SURE.

GAB GAB

W-WHAT'S GOING ON OVER HERE?

IT FEELS LIKE WE'RE ON THE VERGE OF A BREAKTHROUGH!

G-GENIUS!!

GASP

"FOR INSTANCE, WE COULD ADD PICTURES OR DESCRIPTIONS TO THE MENU ITEMS."

"YOU ALL WORKED HARD ON THIS PLAN, SO LET'S JUST FIND A WAY TO MAKE IT SHINE."

ONLY TWO AVAILABLE MOVES

BECOMES CONFUSED WHEN HIS OPPONENT IS TOO WEAK TO START WITH.

MONOMA
HP: 89
MP: 248
EXP: 21

MOVES
SNARK
▷ STANDBY

WHY'S MONOMA JUST SITTING THERE LIKE A LUMP...?

SOMETHING'S OFF...

GASP

GOLDFISH   MOCHI

THE HODGE-PODGE MOTIF ISN'T TOO OUT OF CHARACTER FOR CLASS A BUT USUALLY THEY SHOW MORE UNITY.

THEM? NOT HERE. THEY'VE GOT INTERNSHIPS...

WHERE ARE BAKUGO AND MIDORIYA?

BINGO!!

I-I'M WILLING TO PAY.

COMING RIGHT UP, MA'AM!

HUH? WHY?

C-COULD YOU...DO SOME IMPRESSIONS OF THEM... FOR ME?

GIFT HORSE'S MOUTH

THE PILLAR MEN RETURN

"AND GOLLY GEE, SINCE IT'S SUMMER, WHY DOESN'T TODOROKI MAKE SOME SHAVED ICE?"

"SERVE THE CUSTOMERS SOME DAMN TEA, AT LEAST!! YOU TRYING TO MAKE 'EM PARCHED?!"

GASP GASP

I'M KINDA JEALOUS, ACTUALLY ...

FLOWERS ARE DESTINED TO WILT.

WELL, THAT'S THAT.

THAT CLASS IS LIKE A BOUQUET WITH SOME REAL STANDOUT FLOWERS...

WHAT? ARE THOSE TWO THE MAIN CHARACTERS OR SOMETHING...?

RIGHT! IT'S ALL CUZ THOSE TWO HAVEN'T BEEN AROUND!

AMAZING!! THIS IS TOTALLY SNAPPING US OUTTA OUR FUNK AND SOLVING ALL OUR PROBLEMS !!

THANKS A LOT! WITHOUT YOU, WE WOULD'VE BEEN DEAD IN THE WATER.

HEY, KENDO!

NO BIG DEAL.

TMP TMP TMP

UGH...

WOW, THIS IS GREAT!

ARGH! WE WERE SO CLOSE!

I'M ALL... OUTTA MP FOR THIS MOVE...

WHAT'S WRONG, OCHA-GO?!

SORRY, RIGHT... THANKS, I GUESS.

WE THREW IN A DISCOUNT ON THE IMPRESSIONS.

OH, AND YOUR BILL! THAT'LL BE 1,200 YEN.

KENDO STARTED TO SEE CLASS A AS RIVALS THAT DAY.

*ABOUT $12

THEY'RE BACK!! THE REAL ONES!!

AT LAST, OUR TWO MISSING PIECES!!

TANABATA FESTIVAL? I WISH I COULD'VE HELPED OUT...

I SEE OUR CLASS WENT WITH THE CLASSIC "HAUNTED CAFE," HUH?

42

CHILD OF THE ABYSS

WHOA!

WHO'S YOUR LITTLE FRIEND, TOKOYAMI?

GRAB

ARGH—URK!!

DAMN YOU, TOKOYAMI!!!

WHAAAT?! IS THAT DARK SHADOW?!

YOU'RE ANNOYING.

TUG

IT'S MINETA'S DREAM, BASICALLY...

SO A VILLAIN'S QUIRK DID THIS? TEMPORARILY?!

EXACTLY! *MY* DREAM! SO WHY DOES *HE* GET TO ENJOY IT?!

FUMIKAGE TOKOYAMI

QUIRK: DARK SHADOW

HE HARBORS A SHADOWY YET CORPOREAL FAMILIAR INSIDE HIS BODY THAT CAN EMERGE AND RETRACT AT WILL.

DARK SHADOW

TOKOYAMI'S RELIABLE BUDDY. IT'S GOT A MIND OF ITS OWN, AND WHEN THE LIGHTS GO OUT, IT OFTEN STARTS RAMPAGING!!

THE ADVENTURES OF TOKOYAMI: OBEY, DARK SHADOW!!

NO. 84!!

APPLE FALLS FAR FROM THE TREE

WHAT THE ?!

BAM

HEY!

EVERYBODY SAY HEY !!

AH... I SEE. VERY WELL DONE.

FUMIKAGE.

SKCH SKCH

BADUM

WAHH ...

JOLT

STOP BOTHERING HIM.

AWW, TODOROKI !!

...

RIGHT. SORRY.

NO NEED TO BE THAT STRICT.

DON'T ENCOURAGE IT.

I DON'T MIND. REALLY.

RESTRAINING ORDER

SO YOU ENCOUNTERED A QUIRK THAT TURNS OTHER QUIRKS INTO HUMAN FORMS?

WANNA GO SOMEWHERE DARK.

SO IT'S JUST A VISUAL CHANGE, IN YOUR CASE?

UNCLEAR.

MOST LIKELY.

TUG TUG

VICE

WHY DON'TCHA COME ALONG WITH ME? I WON'T DO ANYTHING NASTY TO YA.

GO AWAY, PERV BOY.

OH HO, KEEP IT COMING.

COCKROACH POOP.

SOMEPLACE DARK, EVEN.

PANT PANT

PANT

AMAZING... SO YOUNG, YET ALREADY SO PERFECT!! I WONDER HOW SHE'LL BE IN TEN YEARS?

THIS IS GETTING US NOWHERE. CAN SOMEONE TIE HIM UP IN THE YARD?

DURRR

DASH

SO WHAT CAN WE DO TO HELP?

FLUFFY HEAD.

JUST ACT NORMALLY, PLEASE.

IF YOU SAY SO...

44

MISTER SHOTA	GREEN SCAPEGOAT

THAT'S IT FOR TODAY.

N-NEVER THOUGHT WE'D LIVE TO SEE THAT...

...BUT I STILL AIN'T SHOWING MERCY!!

YOUR THING MIGHT HAVE A GIRLIE FACE NOW...

DRY EYE

LIKE COTTON CANDY.

ERASURE

TWILIGHT CLAWS

NATURALLY.

BLACK ABYSSAL BODY

I APOLOGIZE. IT'S ACTING OUT BECAUSE EVERYONE'S BEEN SPOILING IT.

TOKOYAMI. CONTROL YOUR QUIRK.

EEK!

HUH?!

DARK SHADOW!! RETURN!!

NUH-UH!

UGH...

BAKUGO BROKE!!

ARGH... WHY ME?!

DEKU!!

HOWITZER IMPACT!!

45

CHAOS UNLEASHED

YIKES. SOMEONE SMASHED THE CIRCUIT BREAKER?

AS I TOLD YOU PEOPLE...

OH NO...

HUSH

BOW DOWN!!

YES, M'LADY!!

MWAH HAH HA!

SHADOWNIA'S ALMIGHTY!!

...ONLY DISCORD AND DESTRUCTION AWAIT...

THAT'S "GODDESS SHADOWNIA" TO YOU!!

GAH!

GRAB

HNGH

CALM YOURSELF, DARK SHADOW!!

YUP.

MM-HMM.

NO... STAY BACK!

DASH

TOKOYAMI WAS RIGHT. WE GOTTA SUBDUE THAT THING.

DECENT WHEN IT DOESN'T COUNT

STOP!

MEANIE-HEAD.

DARK SHADOW IS WEAK TO LIGHT SOURCES!!

SAVE YOUR SYMPATHY. IT ISN'T HUMAN.

BAM

UM, IS THAT REALLY NECESSARY?

WHEN THAT'S THROWN OFF, ALL THAT AWAITS IS DISCORD AND DESTRUCTION.

OUR RELATIONSHIP OF TRUST IS BASED ON THE CLEAR-CUT HIERARCHY BETWEEN US.

THE LAST THING IT NEEDS IS A WEIRD NAME!!

RUN, SHADOWNIA!!

GET AWAY FROM HER!

SLAM

BAM

MINETA, YOU FOOL...

UGH!

EPILOGUE OF DARKNESS

I'M SURE GLAD THAT'S OVER!!

CHIRP

CHIRP

GOOD JOB CLEANING UP, SHADOWNIA.

SHADOWNIA'S HELPING!!

TMP TMP TMP TMP

TH-THANKS.

SORRY ABOUT RUINING YOUR OTHER ONE.

HERE'S A NEW NOTEBOOK.

MADE BY MOMO →

SHP

Dark Shadow Chapter Hierarchy
1. Tokoyami
2. Todoroki
3. Bakugo
4. Shadownia
5. Momoyao
.
.
.
1058. Cockroach poop
1059. Mineta

YEAH?! YOU WANNA RUMBLE?!

IMMA BEAT YOU THIS TIME!!

ROAR

BIRD AS GOOD AS HIS WORD

!!

THIS IS *MY* TRIAL TO OVERCOME.

HNNGH

UNDERSTAND? I ASK THAT YOU STAY BACK.

TOKOYAMI...

AND IT'S ABOUT WHAT LIES AHEAD TOO.

IT'S HOW I'VE COME THIS FAR.

GRAB

HN

NGH

GOT YOU.

I AM THE MASTER!!

NOW OBEY, DARK SHADOW...

ABYSS

MEZO SHOJI

WHAT'S THIS MYSTERIOUS BOY'S FACE REALLY LOOK LIKE?! HE DOESN'T GET MUCH PANEL TIME SINCE HE RARELY ASSERTS HIMSELF, BUT HE'S A KEY CHARACTER WHO ROUNDS OUT THE VARIED CLASS A LINEUP.

WHEN THE CLASS STARTS GOING NUTS, SHOJI WILL REACH OUT TO WHOEVER'S FEELING LEFT OUT... HE'S A NICE GUY IN THAT SENSE. I HEARD A RUMOR THAT THE DATA BOOK REVEALS HIS TRUE FACE (?)...

YUGA AOYAMA

THE SPARKLY NARCISSIST WHO CLAIMS TO HAVE NOBLE ORIGINS!! UNLIKE SHOJI, HE ASSERTS HIMSELF PLENTY, WHICH MAKES IT ALL THE MORE PATHETIC THAT HE BARELY GETS ANY PANEL TIME EITHER!!

IF IT'S ALL THE SAME TO YOU, JUST IMAGINE THAT IN EVERY SCENE, HE'S STRIKING SOME RIDICULOUS POSE OFF-PANEL AND STARING DIRECTLY INTO THE CAMERA!!

WHEN HE'S IGNORED LIKE THAT, HIS SPARKLING BEAUTY REALLY SHINES!!

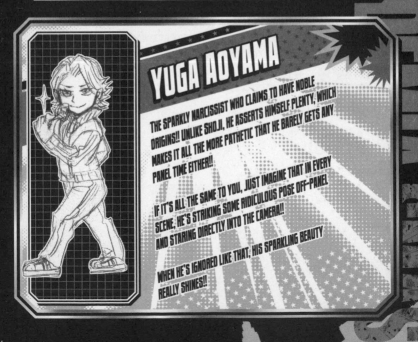

SHUT-IN'S WOE

ARGH... TOO HOT. DYING.

PANT

BLAZE

PANT

WHY A MOUNTAIN...? WHY NOT AN INDOOR POOL?

SUNLIGHT GIVES YOU THAT ESSENTIAL VITAMIN D!

TMP

TMP

OH HO HO, THAT WOULDN'T DO AT ALL.

UGH...

LAMBAST ME ALL YOU LIKE. I CAN TAKE IT.

LISTEN. IF I COLLAPSE, YOU'RE GONNA PAY...

GAHHH, TOO HOT!!

WHAT A NUT-CASE. Like always.

I... DIDN'T MEAN TO...

MUTTER MUTTER

FATHER... I'M SORRY.

SMAK

I'M DONE!!

MUTTER MUTTER

OH NO.

NO. 85!!

AT KUROGIRI'S SUGGESTION, THE LEAGUE OF VILLAINS IS HAVING A GROUP TRAINING EXERCISE IN THE GREAT OUTDOORS.

THIS GANG OF LAZY HOMEBODIES IS TASKED WITH CLIMBING THE HOLY (?) MT. TAKAO (599 METERS).

MT. TAKAO

MT. FUJI

3776 m

599 m

AND THEN THERE WERE SIX

THIS DOESN'T EVEN COUNT AS REAL MOUNTAIN-CLIMBING!

OH?

YOU GUYS ARE ALL PATHETIC!!

8848m

3776m

599m

HUH?

THAT'S A BIT FAR. I COULD MANAGE MT. FUJI...

GREAT. DO IT.

KUROGIRI, WARP THIS TOUGH GUY TO EVEREST.

ZRRRM

I'LL SEND HIM TO THE 5TH STATION.

HANG ON! I'M SORRY...

WHOA! WAIT!! JUST ME? ALONE?! NOOO...

TAKE LOTS OF NICE PICTURES FOR US.

MT. FUJI 5TH STATION

WAI—

ZRM ZRM

HMM?

OOH. POPULAR DESTINATION...

ACTUALLY, SHOULD WE JOIN HIM ON FUJI?

HAR HAR, FUNNY. BUT NO.

BURNING LOVE

EVERY-THING OKAY, SWEET DABI?

I'VE GOT... METABOLISM ISSUES.

FRET FRET

I'M FEELING THE HEAT TOO, THOUGH...

I SHOULD PROBABLY KEEP MY HAND IN THERE TO BE SURE!!

NO, THAT'S REALLY NOT NECESSARY.

GRAB

FLOP FLOP

OH DEAR!! YOU'RE BURNING UP ALL OVER!!

LISTEN, MAGNE. JUST WORRY ABOUT YOURSELF AND LEAVE ME ALONE, OKAY?

GLARE

NO THANKS.

HOW ABOUT SOME BARLEY TEA? I BREWED IT MYSELF!

IT'LL COOL YOU DOWN...

OKAY. BUT I'M YOURS FOR LIFE.

NOD NOD NOD

???

50

"LOVE" QUADRANGLE

WHINING JUST BURNS MORE ENERGY. KEEP QUIET.

I'M DONE...

WHY, WE AREN'T EVEN HALFWAY.

HO HO HO

PANT

PANT

HOW ABOUT... SOME CHILLED BARLEY TEA?

THROAT'S SO DRY... ON FIRE.

NO...

SKCH SKCH

SKCH

HEH.

HOW RUDE!

UNLESS YOU'VE GOT STORE-BOUGHT! CUZ WHEN PEOPLE BREW IT AT HOME, IT ALWAYS SMELLS FUNKY!

ACTUALLY AGREES

I WILL HAPPILY PARTAKE.

REFRESHING!! NOTHING TOPS BARLEY TEA ON A HOT SUMMER'S DAY.

PWAHH!

GULP GULP

GULP

SO NOT MY TYPE! BUT HE'S SO MANLY!

BATTY BLADES

MEAT... FLESH...

YOU'RE ALL SO SLOW!

THNK

THNK

TEETH FUNCTION AS LEGS SURPRISINGLY WELL

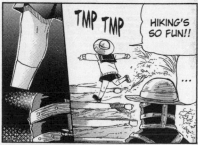

TMP TMP

HIKING'S SO FUN!!

...

BUT IT'S HARD TO RESIST GOING ALL STABBY-STABBY.

I FEEL SO AT HOME WITH THE LEAGUE...

?!

AHH... ERR...

WHOAAA ?!

SHNK SHNK

MEAT!! MEEEAT!!

SHNK

SHNK

SHNK

SEND THOSE WACKOS AWAY TOO, KUROGIRI ...!

51

CARB MOTIVATION

WE CAN ENJOY OUR SENSE OF ACCOMPLISHMENT WITH DELICIOUS BOWLS OF NOODLES.

NICE. I'M DOWN.

I HEAR THERE'S A SOBA SHOP AT THE PEAK.

NEVER MIND HIM. LET'S GO.

BNNN BNNN BNNN

HAH.

THEY *WISH* I'D JOIN THEM...

STUPID CICADAS.

BNNN BNNN

SO... STINKIN' HOT...

SO THIRSTY. WANNA GO HOME.

BBNNN

MRMR MRMR

I'LL GO, BUT ONLY TO ESCAPE THE NOISE.

AND HE'LL WARP ME HOME IF HE KNOWS WHAT'S GOOD FOR HIM.

STUPID...

THAT'S WHY. YUP.

PARTICIPATION TROPHY

BAM

OH.

THE PEAK, AT LAST.

NOPE. DON'T CARE. I SAY THIS IS THE PEAK.

IT'S NOT UP TO YOU!!

NO, THIS IS JUST AN OBSERVATION DECK.

WHETHER THE PEAK'S HERE OR THERE, WE'VE STILL ACCOMPLISHED NOTHING!

THE VALUE IS IN THE JOURNEY, TOMURA SHIGARAKI!

YAP YAP

SHUT UP!! OUR ONLY REWARD FOR CLIMBING THIS DUMB ROCK IS GETTING TO WALK BACK DOWN!!

DO YOU ARGUE JUST TO HEAR YOURSELF TALK?

BOOM. MIC DROP.

GRR GRR

NOPE. ONLY TANGIBLE RESULTS MATTER. EVEN LITTLE KIDS STOP CARING ABOUT PATS ON THE BACK SOONER OR LATER.

LEAGUE OF TOURISTS

KRK KRK KRK

WHAT'S WRONG WITH YOU?

PERHAPS I OVERDID IT WITH THAT HIKE YESTERDAY?

URGH...

IT SEEMS I DID A NUMBER ON MY BACK...

HA HA HA HA! SERVES YOU RIGHT.

HEH HEH. MUST SUCK BEING AN OLD GEEZER!!

SLAM SLAM SLAM

NOW GIMME A GINGER ALE.

SHIGA-RAKI...

Y-YES OF COURSE. JUST A MOMENT.

THEY CLEARLY ENJOYED THEIR TIME ON MT. FUJI.

WHO'RE THOSE FOREIGNERS?

BZZ BZZ BZZ

DROP IT. I'M NEVER STEPPING FOOT ON A MOUNTAIN AGAIN.

SYNCHRONICITY

THAT GROSS CRAP? MAKES ME BREAK OUT IN HIVES.

YOU DIDN'T WANT TO ORDER GRATED YAM?

Why so close?

HEH. Another thing in common

THERE'S NOTHING LIKE A GOOD MEAL AFTER HARD EXERCISE.

MM, SCRUMP-TIOUS! WHAT DO YOU THINK, SHIGARAKI?

TASTES... THE SAME AS EVER.

...BUT DOESN'T THIS INSPIRE YOU TO GET OUT THERE AND BE THE BADDEST YOU CAN BE?

NOW, I KNOW YOU'VE HAD TROUBLE COMING UP WITH EVIL PLANS LATELY...

SHUT UP AND EAT.

THAT'S DUMB. WARP US.

I THOUGHT WE MIGHT RETURN VIA THE CABLE CAR?

ALSO, YOU'RE WARPING US HOME...

OOH, THAT SOUNDS FUN.

JINX.

53

ANOTHER HERO ACADEMIA

WHY'RE YOU SCARED? WE GO TO U.A., FOR PETE'S SAKE.

YEAH, BUT STILL...

WHAT'RE THESE SHIKETSU DUDES DOING HERE?

SIR, YES, SIR!!

BAM

OUR VISITORS HAVE BEEN GOING AROUND TO OTHER SCHOOLS TO LEARN MORE.

SHIKETSU HIGH SCHOOL!!

IF YOU'RE HOPING TO BE A HERO, YOU'D HAVE TO BE LIVING UNDER A ROCK NOT TO HAVE HEARD THAT NAME!!

IF IT'S U.A. IN THE EAST, IT'S SHIKETSU IN THE WEST!!

YES, SHIKETSU'S ANOTHER FAMOUS ACADEMY THAT PUMPS OUT PLENTY OF SUPERHEROES!! THEY'RE ALSO KNOWN FOR BEING NUTS ABOUT DISCIPLINE!!

TEACH US WHAT IT'S ALL ABOUT!!

REALLY, DID THEY HAVE TO BE WEIRDOS?

WE'VE COME TO THIS STANDOUT ACADEMY TO LEARN WHAT MAKES IT THE BEST OF THE BEST!!

WE OFTEN GO WITHOUT SEATS AS PART OF OUR TRAINING.

THAT'S NICE, BUT YOU'RE IN MY WAY.

FWP

NO, THIS IS FINE.

THERE ARE SOME DESKS AT THE BACK YOU CAN USE.

ALREADY STALE

SLAM

TOMP

TOMP

OW!

HAGAKURE IS INVISIBLE. BE MORE CAREFUL.

???

HMM?!

THAT'S TOTALLY MY BAD!!

AND NOW YOU'RE STOMPING ON OJIRO'S TAIL...

FWIP

I'LL BE SURE TO WATCH MYSELF!!

STOMP

ACK!!

YOW!!

WE'VE NEVER MET SUCH A ONE-NOTE CHARACTER BEFORE!

BONK

I'M SUPER-DUPER SORRY!!

GAH!

RELATABLE

MY HOBBY IS SPENDING MY DAYS EMBODYING THE PRIDE AND DIGNITY OF SHIKETSU HIGH SCHOOL.

I AM SEIJI SHISHIKURA, A SECOND-YEAR AT SHIKETSU HIGH SCHOOL!!

BAM

I LOVE EVERYTHING HOT AND HOT-BLOODED!! THINK OF ME AS YOUR NEW BEST PAL!

SLAM

AND I'M INASA YOARASHI, A FIRST-YEAR AT SHIKETSU!!

172cm

190cm

INASA... I'VE TOLD YOU BEFORE—DON'T STAND IN FRONT OF ME...

AH!! PARDON ME!!

YIKES...

THEY'RE ALL ABOUT SHIKETSU PRIDE! WE'LL NEVER GET ALONG...

BONK

LET ME JUST BOW AGAIN, THEN...

PHEW

OWW!!

BUT WE'VE GOT A SOFT SPOT FOR IDIOTS.

UGH, JOCKS

FASCINATING.

THIS IS THE BUS TO OUR TRAINING GROUNDS!!

HUH? MAYBE THESE GUYS ARE OKAY!!

BADUM

Sounds fun!!

TRAINING, IS IT? THEN WE WILL RUN ALONGSIDE YOUR BUS.

HUSH

SURE ARE A LOTTA ATHLETIC TYPES IN OUR CLASS.

TMP TMP TMP TMP

JUST A BIT FARTHER, EVERYONE!

SAME THING BOTH SIDES

CARE TO SHOW ME SOME OF THAT U.A. PRIDE?

STARE

UGH. I HATE THIS TYPE OF GUY THE MOST.

I VALUE TRADITION AND HIERARCHY MORE THAN ANYTHING.

LIKE, YOU BOTH PLAY MUSIC...

THAT DOESN'T COUNT FOR MUCH!!

HE'S THE SAME TYPE AS YOU, JIRO.

HUH?! HOW SO?!

THE WEIRD SORT OF MASOCHIST WHO CAN'T TAKE A BREATH UNLESS THE RULES SAY HE CAN.

I'M ALL ABOUT LIVING FREE!! HE'S THE OPPOSITE!!

DUNNO WHAT ANY OF THAT MEANS, BUT WOW, THEY REALLY ARE ALIKE...

OH YEAH? WELL I SAY FASCIST IDEOLOGUES LIKE YOU ARE WHAT'S WRONG WITH SOCIETY TODAY.

YAP YAP

LISTEN, ICONOCLAST! SOCIETY WOULD CEASE TO FUNCTION WITHOUT LAW AND ORDER!

A LOT OF HOT AIR

UNEXPECTED COMPATIBILITY

LESSER OF TWO EVILS

INASA!! HOW DARE YOU INJURE THE INSTRUCTOR!!

DON'T "OOPS" ME!!

OOPS!

THANKS SO MUCH FOR TODAY!! WE LEARNED A WHOLE LOT!!

OUCH!!

DON'T STRIKE ME TOO HARD, PLEASE!

IT'S FINE. CUT THAT OUT.

WE'VE DISHONORED OUR SCHOOL! IN THE NAME OF SHIKETSU, I, SHISHIKURA, WILL ACCEPT PUNISHMENT!

I SAID, FORGET IT. IF YOU'VE GOT TIME TO APOLOGIZE, SPEND IT ON SOMETHING MORE PRODUCTIVE!

THANK YOU, SIR!!

15 MINUTES LATER

Q-QUIET. IT'S TIME FOR HOME-ROOM.

WHAT'S THAT FACE MEAN, SENSEI?

I'M POOPED.

To repent, we shall go home on foot!

SUDDENLY, THE USUAL SUSPECTS DIDN'T SEEM HALF-BAD.

YOARASHI BY WEST, MIDORIYA BY EAST

I THINK I KNOW...

I DON'T GET WHAT'S LIKABLE ABOUT HIM.

NAW, YOU'RE ALL AWE-SOME!!

BLAH BLAH

YOU'RE AWESOME, DUDE!!

OH... I GUESS HE CAN BE FUNNY ONCE IN A WHILE.

HA HA HA

THE OTHER PROS PROBABLY SEE ALL MIGHT THAT WAY, SOMETIMES.

IN A WAY...IT REMINDS ME OF YOU TOO.

SAY WHAT?!

YES, EXACTLY.

AND, LIKE... EVEN IF HE GOT US CAUGHT UP IN THAT WIND, HE STILL MANAGED TO SAVE EVERYONE.

AND YOU'RE THE GLOOMY VERSION.

B-BUT ALL MIGHT'S GLOOMIER THAN YOU KNOW.

HE'S LIKE THE DUMBER VERSION OF ALL MIGHT.

SHOTO IN A PINCH

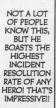

THE CURRENT NUMBER TWO HERO, ENDEAVOR!!

NOT A LOT OF PEOPLE KNOW THIS, BUT HE BOASTS THE HIGHEST INCIDENT RESOLUTION RATE OF ANY HERO! THAT'S IMPRESSIVE!!

TODAY, ONE OF THE TOP CURRENT HEROES WILL BE YOUR GUEST LECTURER!!

NO. 87!!

WHOA... KEEP IT TOGETHER, TODOROKI!

IT DOESN'T HURT.

SKWEEZ

SKWEEZ SKWEEZ

STOP PINCHING YOURSELF, MAN!!

I SAW THE KIND OF WEAK LESSONS YOU'RE GETTING HERE (SEE NO. 76)!! SO I'M HERE TO TRAIN YOU KIDDOS MYSELF.

SHOCK

?!

THE ADVENTURES OF TODOROKI: FILIAL PIETY OR BUST?

SHUDDER

E-ENDEAVOR?!

SHOTO!! NOT ONLY HAVE YOU BEEN AVOIDING HOME, YOU'VE IGNORED MY PHONE CALLS AND TEXTS!!

UNACCEPTABLE!!

9/11 How've you been?
10/2 Hey
12/18 What's going on...
3/5 Cancelled
     Did something happen?

DO YOU HAVE ANY CLUE HOW THAT'S MADE ME FEEL?

YOU'RE ABOUT TO FIND OUT!!

BWOOM

THE WAY HE NEVER LOVED ME

GATHERING INTEL ON THE SCENE IS THE MOST IMPORTANT JOB THERE IS.

TH-THANKS?

GREAT QUIRK YOU'VE GOT THERE.

ONCE YOU REFINE THOSE SKILLS, YOU'LL BE A VALUED TEAM MEMBER.

HONESTLY, HE'S A WAY BETTER TEACHER THAN ALL MIGHT.

YEAH, HE'S ON FIRE TODAY.

HUH. MAYBE HE'S NOT THE TOTAL JERKHOLE WE THOUGHT HE WAS.

SO HE CAN EMPATHIZE WITH OUR STRUGGLES!!

The compliment knocked some screws loose

THAT'S BECAUSE ENDEAVOR CLIMBED THE LADDER OF SUCCESS THROUGH SHEER EFFORT!

MIDORIYA...

HEH HEH.

NO PROBLEMO!

ENDEAVOR SENSEI! INSTRUCT ME HOW TO WIELD MY QUIRK AS WELL!!

GRRR

GLANCE

I-I SEE YOUR GAME!!

DADLIEST SCHEME

OH MY, THERE SURE ARE SOME *RUDE CHILDREN* IN THIS CLASS. ANYONE WHO DOESN'T WANT TO BE HERE SHOULD *GO HOME.*

ALL RIGHT. WHAT'S THE BIG IDEA?!

GRR!

H-HIYA, I'M MIDORIYA.

SEE NO. 59!!

OH. YOU'RE A FAMILIAR FACE.

KEEPING MY BOOTS WARM FOR ME?

HMPH. I SEE YOU'RE MOVING THOSE HIPS A LOT BETTER NOWADAYS!

SKWIRM SKWIRM

YOU BET!! I EVEN WORE 'EM A FEW TIMES!!

AW, YOU NOTICED?!

BOOTS?

SMART THINKING! I'VE GOT A GREAT TRAINING PROGRAM FOR YOU, IN THAT CASE.

YAP YAP

I'VE ACTUALLY BEEN TRAINING MY LEGS LATELY, TO GIVE ME MORE ATTACK OPTIONS!!

I call it Shoot Style!!

NEVER TRUST ANYONE...

BACKFIRING

SENSEI!! OBSERVE MY FORM!

COMING ALONG NICELY!

HOW'D I LOOK JUST NOW, ENDEAVOR?!

WAIT YOUR TURN.

HMM?

HEH HEH... WHAT NOW, SHOTO? YOU'LL COME CRAWLING BACK TO ME SOON ENOUGH...

ENDY! ENDER! ENDEAVOR!! ENDES?!

RMBL

SHO—

BA

M!!

SHOTOOO?!

PETTY MIGHT

GRR! TALK ABOUT ADDING INSULT TO INJURY!!

AH HA HEH HEH!

YAP YAP

RIP

ESPECIALLY MIDORIYA... HE WAS SO SUPPORTIVE AT THE SPORTS FESTIVAL, BUT NOW...

ENDEAVOR IS MY FAVORITE!!

*Didn't actually say that

YOUR POWER ...IS YOUR OWN!!

RIP

A-ALL MIGHT?!

I KNOW HOW YOU MUST FEEL...

That poor telephone pole...

GLOOM

LOOM

PSST. KID...

HOW ABOUT WE DO SOME TRAINING TOGETHER?

Weak lessons!

Better than All Might!

I love Endeavor!!

*Didn't actually say that

GLOOM GLOOM

IN TRUTH, I HAVE MY OWN REASONS FOR BEING UNHAPPY WITH THIS.

SYMPATHY FOR THE DEVIL

I HAVE TO CHECK IN WITH FUYUMI TO MAKE SURE YOU'RE EVEN STILL ALIVE. THINK ABOUT MY FEELINGS FOR ONCE!!

I STARTED A 'LINE' ACCOUNT JUST TO MESSAGE YOU, BUT YOU'VE LEFT THOSE MESSAGES AS "UNREAD" FOR HALF A YEAR NOW!!

UNREAD FOR SIX MONTHS? THAT'S COLD, MAN.

WAIT, IS THAT TRUE?

AW, ENDEAVOR.

DASH

UGH...

I-IT'S LIKE I DON'T KNOW YOU ANY-MORE!!

I THOUGHT YOU WERE POKING FUN AT MY TERRIBLE TEACHING STYLE, YET...

E-ENDEAVOR... I SEE WHAT WAS MOTIVATING THIS, NOW.

FEELS GUILTY

USE YOUR HEAD! MORE MEDDLING'S ONLY GONNA MAKE IT WORSE!

DON'T!!

I-I'D BETTER GO APOLOGIZE TO ENDEAVOR!

OH...? YOU THINK?

FATHER FIGURE

W-WHAT'RE YOU DOING WITH HIM ANYWAY?!

SPARK. SPARK. SPARK.

Y-YOU!! WIPE THAT GRIN OFF YOUR FACE!!

SHOTOOO!!

OH, NOTH-ING MUCH.

YOU'RE THE ONE WHO TOLD UNWILLING PARTICIPANTS TO JUST LEAVE.

BUT YOU ARE WILLING! I SEE THAT SWEAT!!

HA HA

ENOUGH!! THIS IS MY LESSON!! YOU LISTEN TO ME!!

BUDDY-BUDDY? NAW. JUST TRAINING.

EXPLAIN THE FIST BUMP, THEN!!

Oh my.

FLUSTERED

Y-YOU IGNORE ALL MY TEXTS... YET NOW YOU'RE BUDDY-BUDDY WITH THIS OVERIN-FLATED CHUMP?!

62

THROWN BONE

THIS JOB IS ROUGH WITHOUT ENDEAVOR AROUND...

SURE HOPE HE COMES BACK SOON.

TAKING A HALF-DAY

TCH...

ENDEAVOR, YOU'RE BACK!!

BAM

GREET-INGS, USELESS SIDE-KICKS!!

BWOOOM

WHAT'S THE SITCH?

SHADDUP!! I SAID, GIMME AN UPDATE!!

ROAR

WHY'RE YOUR EYES SO RED? YOU BEEN CRYING OR SOME-THING?!

I CAN'T.

NOPE. TOO MUCH...

FWUMP

You receiving these?

Stop worrying about me.

BA-DUM

He read but didn't respond!

...

ALL IN

TODOROKI HAS HIS REASONS, SO I THINK WE SHOULD TRUST HIM ON THIS.

YEAH. EVEN IF YOU DON'T REALLY GET ALONG.

YOU OUGHTA TEXT YOUR DAD BACK, MAN.

MIDORIYA ...

SOOO... GIMME HIS NUMBER?

MIDO-RIYA !!! ....

IN WHICH CASE...I COULD HANDLE ENDEAVOR FOR YOU?

REAL CLASSY! WE'RE OUT HERE WORRYING ABOUT THIS DUDE'S RELATION-SHIP WITH HIS DAD!!

WHO? ME? NO.

JOLT

YOU JUST WANNA TEXT WITH A PRO HERO!!

YOU GUYS...

YOU GUYS ...?

HELPING A DUDE AND HIS DAD RECONCILE GETS ME FIRED UP!!

EXCITED

SOOO... LET US COMPOSE THOSE TEXTS FOR YOU?

SKIMPING ON DETAILS

AND PRESS CONFERENCES ARE GAUNTLETS THAT CAN SEE YOUR REPUTATION RISE...OR FALL!

DEALING WITH THE MEDIA CAN BE LIFE-OR-DEATH FOR HEROES!

OUR CURRICULUM IS ALL ABOUT THESE PRAGMATIC, HANDS-ON EXPERIENCES.

THE U.A. HERO COURSE IS NEVER ONE TO SKIMP ON THESE DETAILS.

SUCKING ALL THE FUN OUT, HUH.

PRESS CONFERENCE

WE'LL EACH GIVE YOU UP TO 25 POINTS, FOR A MAXIMUM TOTAL OF 100!!

JUDGING YOU WILL BE US FOUR, WHO HAVE PLENTY OF PRACTICE HANDLING THE MEDIA!!

HANG ON!! YOU NEED TO TELL US THE SCENARIO, AT LEAST!

GO, GO, GO! PLUS ULTRA!!

OH YEAH. OOPS.

NO. 88!!

YOU KIDS HAVE ENDURED ALL SORTS OF TRAINING UP TO NOW...

...BUT YOU'LL NEVER GUESS WHAT WE'RE DOING TODAY!!

ALL MIGHT

ERM... ULTIMATE MOVE TRAINING...?

Deku

NOPE!! THE ANSWER IS... PRESS CONFERENCE TRAINING!!

C-COME AGAIN?!

64

MIGHTLIKE

BUL-GE

AHEM!!

DEKU

I'M S'POSED TO BE... "IN CHARACTER"?

UGH. I SUCK AT THESE THINGS. BUT NO... THIS IS ESSENTIAL.

...AND I'M PRONE TO SCREWING UP...

UM, I KNOW I'VE STILL GOT A LOT TO LEARN...

NO, THAT'S NOT RIGHT. I WANT TO BE LIKE HIM, BUT THAT'S NOT IN CHARACTER FOR ME.

I'LL JUST HAVE TO SPEAK FROM THE HEART.

THAT'S WHAT I'M FOCUSING ON, DAY AFTER DAY.

SO I'LL KEEP... TRYING MY BEST.

BUT I WANT TO BE A HERO WHO CAN INSPIRE EVERYONE.

PHEW! I DID BETTER THAN I THOUGHT!!

BRAVO!!

78

GREAT GOING, KID!!

THOUGH YOU SHOULD PROBABLY ADDRESS THE ACTUAL ALLEGATIONS IN SOME FORM.

SETTING THE STANDARD

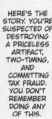

THIS PRESS CONFERENCE IS WHERE YOU GET TO EXPLAIN AND/OR APOLOGIZE.

THAT SOUNDS INTENSE!

HERE'S THE STORY. YOU'RE SUSPECTED OF DESTROYING A PRICELESS ARTIFACT, TWO-TIMING, AND COMMITTING TAX FRAUD. YOU DON'T REMEMBER DOING ANY OF THIS.

THIS IS TRAINING...!?

What's your relationship with Pirate Queen?!

UM...

ONE EXPLOSION MURDER CTBA

THAT'S ALL! BYE!!

ROAR

I DON'T REMEMBER A SINGLE THING!!

WHAAAT?! THAT WAS ACCEPTABLE?!

88

HMPH. VERY MUCH IN CHARACTER.

UPRIGHT AND HONEST, AT LEAST.

22 UWABAMI

21 ALL MIGHT

COMMITMENT

WHITE CLOTHES AND A SHAVED HEAD!!

BAM

THESE ACCUSATIONS AGAINST ME HAPPENED CUZ I'VE BEEN SLACKING OFF!!

Does he know this is just training?

That's extreme...

THE ONLY WAY TO RESPOND IS BY PRODUCING RESULTS!!

ZABAM

THANKS FOR YOUR CONTINUED SUPPORT!!

NOOO!! I SHAVED MY HEAD FOR THIS!!

THAT WAS A BIT MUCH.

IT KINDA SOUNDED LIKE HE WAS CONFESSING TO ALL OF IT...?

43

PRESIDENTIAL GAFF

I AM TRULY SORRY FOR ANY TROUBLE I MAY HAVE CAUSED!!

BOW

THIS TRAINING SHOULD BE A BREEZE!

PRESS CONFERENCES? I'VE WATCHED MY BROTHER DO MANY OF THESE...

I WILL WORK HARD DAY AFTER DAY TO REGAIN YOUR TRUST, SO IN RETURN, I HUMBLY REQUEST YOUR CONTINUED SUPPORT!!

THE ALLEGATIONS AGAINST ME ARE ENTIRELY GROUNDLESS!!

SNAP

SNAP

AS I JUST FINISHED EXPLAINING...

SWEAT

SWEAT

WHO?

ARE YOU MESSING AROUND WITH PIRATE QUEEN?!

HRM? WELL, I...

THAT WAS NO EXPLANATION.

N-NOO!!

DOOM

21

YOU CAN'T LET THE PRESS MAKE YOU PANIC.

AND YOU SHOULD SHOW THEM YOUR FACE NICE AND CLEAR AT ALL TIMES.

P. MIC

UWABAMI

MOMO'S COMPLEX COMPLEX

I HAVE NOTHING TO FEAR BUT FEAR ITSELF!!

GLINT

BREATHE

THIS PRESS CONFERENCE IS WHERE I GET TO DISMISS THE UNTRUE ACCUSATIONS...

DID YOU REALLY FABRICATE A FALSE SIDEKICK TO PERPETRATE TAX FRAUD?!

RAHH

EEK...

YOU WERE SEEN ENTERING ADULT KING'S PENTHOUSE!!

WHAT'D YOU DO UP IN THAT PENTHOUSE?!

FRET FRET

NO, I... WELL... I...

UM, UM...

UMM...

WHY DID YOU BLAME A VILLAIN FOR DESTROYING THE ARTIFACT?

CREATY

SHE CRUMBLES UNDER PRESSURE...

THE OPPOSITE OF FROG GIRL...

FLUNK

I DID IT. IT'S ALL TRUE.

SHE CONFESSED!!

FROPPY: MEDIA DARLING

DID YOU REALLY DESTROY THAT PRICELESS ARTIFACT, FROPPY?!

SNAP SNAP

RIBBIT...

FROPPY

WHAT ABOUT THE RUMORS ABOUT YOU AND ADULT KING?

...MAKES ME SO, SO SAD.

FIDGET

UH.

EVEN BEING ACCUSED OF THESE THINGS...

NONE OF THAT...IS EVEN CLOSE TO TRUE.

THE REPORTERS ARE STUNNED SILENT!!

HUSH

RIBBIT RIBBIT

BUT I'LL DO MY BEST TO ANSWER ANY QUESTIONS YOU HAVE.

RIBBIT?

GAB GAB

95

23 P. MIC

25 UWABAMI

THE GIRL'S A PRODIGY.

I'VE NEVER SEEN SOMEONE MAKE REPORTERS CRY.

PALE IMITATION

I SEE... BETTER TO BE HATED THAN HAVE THEM NOT CARE AT ALL?

PEOPLE SEE ME AS A FLAKE ALREADY, SO TRYING TO BE POPULAR IS PROBABLY A LOSING BATTLE.

FWIP

GLINT

SO I'LL TAKE A PAGE OUTTA MINETA'S BOOK!!

YO, MY PEEPS.

HE'S PIGGYBACKING OFF THE LAST ONE?

COPYING GRAPE GUY? HAVE YOU NO PRIDE?

NO, WAIT, HANG ON.

THIS IS TOUGHER THAN I THOUGHT.

FIDGET

ARE YOU MOCKING THE MEDIA?

HUH?

URK.

AND WHY'M I THE ONLY ONE WHO GETS A DIFFERENT LINE OF QUESTIONING?!

THAT DAY, KAMINARI LEARNED HOW TOUGH MINETA REALLY IS.

IF YOU'RE GONNA GO FULL SLEAZE, YOU GOTTA COMMIT.

ALL HE ACCOMPLISHED WAS SHOWING HOW SHALLOW HE IS...

5

1

SCANDAL MAGNET

THESE IDIOTS ALL GOT THE WRONG IDEA!!

EXPOSURE IS EVERYTHING, SO I SAY BRING ON THE BAD HEADLINES!!

ARE YOU INTIMATE WITH PIRATE QUEEN?!

MAYBE.

SLAM

DID YOU DESTROY THE ARTIFACT?!

WHO KNOWS?

HUH... THAT WORKED?!

AND THE TAX FRAUD?

86

WHAT?! BUT HOW?!

OOH, YOU'RE CUTE. WHY DON'TCHA SHOW ME YOUR BYLINE?

MINETA...

BEING HATED...IS BETTER THAN OBSCURITY...

SHAAA

86

THE JUDGES HATE TO ADMIT THE TRUTH.

IT'S THE MEDIA'S ETERNAL DILEMMA.

18 21 20

KOJI KODA

A RESERVED, GENTLE INTROVERT. ACTUALLY, I DON'T KNOW MUCH ABOUT KODA AT ALL! SORRY.

WHENEVER THE OTHERS ARE CAUGHT UP IN SOME NONSENSE, HE'LL BE OFF TO THE SIDE. SO I THINK HE'S WELL LIKED? WHEN HE'S ALONE, HE PROBABLY THINKS BACK ON THEIR ANTICS AND HAS A GOOD CHUCKLE... ALSO, HIS VOICE IS REALLY CUTE.

Oh no!

MASHIRAO OJIRO

EVER SINCE THE VILLAINS FORGOT WHO HE WAS IN THE USJ SEQUENCE, THIS UNLUCKY DUDE HAS BEEN *SMASH!!*'S RESIDENT "CHARACTER WITH A REALLY WEAK PRESENCE"!! SORRY, MAN!!

I'VE COME TO WONDER IF HIS MISFORTUNE IS DUE TO POOR TIMING, OR SOMETHING ABOUT THE BOY HIMSELF, DEEP DOWN...

IN THAT SENSE, HE'S THE TYPE OF GUY YOU WANT TO POKE FUN AT.

MOMO EX MACHINA

TRUE. NOT MANY EVENTS THIS YEAR.

ARGH!!

SUMMER'S ALREADY ENDING AND WE DIDN'T GET TO DO SQUAT!!

TALKIN' 'BOUT LIFE WHILE WATCHING THE SUNSET ON THE BEACH.

TALKIN' 'BOUT HOPES AND DREAMS WHILE STARGAZING!

I WANTED ALL THOSE CLICHÉ MOMENTS!

HOW'S JOSTLING ME GONNA HELP?

SHAKE SHAKE

CAMPING, POOLS, BARBE-CUES!! SUMMER'S GONE AND I'LL NEVER GET IT BACK!!

HOW DOES THAT SOUND, LADIES?

DIVINE INTERVEN-TION FROM OUR GOD-DESS!!

UM, WE COULD "CAMP" IN THE COURT-YARD?

SKRTCH

NO. 89!!

SUMMER'S END ROUSES MEMORIES OF THE SEASON.

LIKE OF SPARK-LERS.

BUT ALSO PLENTY OF LAUGHS, DROWNED OUT BY THE CRASHING WAVES.

GENDER RATIO ENFORCEMENT SQUAD

TRYING TO RECLAIM SUMMER, I HEARD.

HUH?! THAT SHOULD MEAN BIKINIS!

WHAT ARE THEY DOING OUT THERE?

YAP

YAP

HANG ON. THEY LEFT BECAUSE IT'S TOO HOT IN THE TENT?

WAAAY TOO HOT IN THERE.

WHOA!

LEAP

OH, HOLD UP!

FWEET!!

EXCUSE ME, LADIES, BUT THIS CHANGES EVERYTHING!

THE LAW SAYS THAT ONCE THE HENHOUSE IS OPEN, YOU GOTTA LET *ALL* THE FOXES IN!

SUMMERS OF THE RICH AND FABULOUS

WOOOO!!

TA DA!!

CREA-TION

EVEN *I'M* KINDA EXCITED.

I'M JUST GLAD I COULD BE OF SERVICE!

SO HOT! BUT THAT'S OKAY!!

FUMP

SUMMERY ITEMS, YOU SAY...?

HOW ABOUT GIVING US SOME MORE SUMMERY ITEMS, DORAEMON!

OH... UM, SURE...

A fountain...

BAM

IT'S A BIT SMALL, BUT WHAT DO YOU THINK?

CREA-TION

71

TODOROKI LIKES NOODLES

YUKATA ARE THE BEST, HUR HUR!!

YUKATA ARE THE BEST!!

WHUU!

I CAN'T BELIEVE THEY PULLED IT OFF.

We lost.

HOW ABOUT A MORE SLIPPERY MEAL?!

THE SLEEVES MAY GET IN THE WAY...

LET'S DO IT IN OUR YUKATA!

WHAT ABOUT THE BARBECUE, THOUGH?

Can I leave yet?

FWP

WHAT'S GOTTEN INTO YOU TWO TODAY?!

Being so useful.

...THE SUMMERY SOMEN SLIDE!!

WE'RE TALKING ABOUT...

BA

BAM

OR I COULD STAY A BIT LONGER ...

I like noodles.

KRAK

YAP

YAP

Moby-Dick or THE WHALE

THE SOUL OF SUMMER

YEAH RIGHT! THESE GUYS'LL JUST TELL US TO PUT ON BIKINIS.

THE NERVE!!

IF YOU WANNA HANG, YOU GOTTA HAVE A SUMMERY CONTRIBUTION.

WHAT HE SAID!! BEHOLD, THE YAMATO SPIRIT THAT RUNS IN OUR BLOOD, INHERITED ACROSS EONS!

FOR A FAIR MAIDEN'S SAKE I WOULD BRAVE THORN AND BRIAR TO PLUCK HER A ROSE

YOU UNDERESTIMATE A GUY'S WILLINGNESS TO GO THE EXTRA MILE FOR A LADY!

WHOA, NOT A BAD IMAGE!

...WHILE YOU FROLIC AND CHASE AFTER DRAGONFLIES!

IMAGINE A WARM WIND BLOWING ACROSS THE RICE PADDIES AT SUNSET ...

BADUM

WOW!! Y-YOU PASS THE TEST.

The yukata was a nice touch...

HELL YEAH!!

YOUR SIDE PROFILE GARBED IN A BREEZY, SUMMER YUKATA.

OR STANDING ON A BRIDGE WHILE YOU WATCH FIREWORKS FROM THE NEXT TOWN OVER.

SMAK

72

WE'VE GOT TEAM SPIRIT, YES WE DO

HMM? MINE FELL FIRST !!

BLOW

WHOEVER'S SPARKLER ASH FALLS TO THE GROUND FIRST HAS TO CLEAN UP DINNER!

CHF

BOTTLE

JOLT

PFFT

AH... HA HA?

WE CAN ALL HELP!!

YEAH. CUZ YOU BOYS OUTDID YOURSELVES TODAY. GRR.

YOU'RE HELPING ME OUT, JIRO?!

AWW, YOU GUYS ROCK !!

So kind of you!!

HANDS UP! NOODLE POLICE

GET READY FOR THE NOODLES TO FLOW!

HERE WE GO!

YAP YAP

Y E A H H H !!

YOU LOT !!

ZOOM

FWEE FWEE FWEE

THERE'S NO NOODLES REACHING US, HUH.

NOPE.

SUMMER IS DELISH !!

GLOOM

YAP YAP

!

IDA, OUR HERO!

THE DOWN-STREAM PARTICI-PANTS NEED NOODLES TOO! BE MINDFUL!

Okaaay.

BUZZKILLS

BZZZZZZZZZ

GAH!! THE SPRINKLERS ARE GOING OFF ON THE UPPER FLOORS!!

KSSHHHH

HE DIDN'T MIND THE KOTATSU THING, BUT...

WHAT DO WE DO?

OH NO. SENSEI MIGHT SHOW UP.

TOMP

AHHH!

MTTR MTTR

HEY.

BUT GETTING ME SOAKED? NUH-UH.

OH GREAT, IT'S THIS GUY!!

DOOM

YOU WANNA MAKE A RACKET DOWN HERE? BE MY FREAKIN' GUESTS.

SUMMER MEMORIES WE WOULDN'T SOON FORGET.

RUN!!

GAH, AND THIS GUY TOO!

WHAT DO YOU THINK YOU'RE DOING?!

ALARMING

HALF HOT

WE DID SQUEEZE A LOT IN.

IT WAS ALL SO MUCH FUN!

Just what I needed!

OH BOY, WE SUMMERED IT UP REAL GOOD RIGHT AT THE LAST MINUTE!!

BZZZZZZZZZZZ

?!

YOU DIDN'T EVEN START YET?!

SHE NEVER LEARNS

YEAHHH!

NOW I'M FINALLY READY TO START MY SUMMER HOMEWORK, ALSO AT THE LAST MINUTE!

BZZZZZZZZ

IS IT CUZ OF THE BONFIRE?

PUT IT OUT NOW!!

DASH

THAT SOUNDS LIKE THE SMOKE ALARM!!

MAN APRON

THAT'S DEEP, AIZAWA

TO GIVE YOU A RANGE OF EXPERIENCES.

UGH!

A SMALL-TOWN EVENT? WHY ME?!

POPULARITY

STRENGTH

SKILLS

WHILE YOU'RE STILL YOUNG, YOU SHOULD BE TRYING DIFFERENT THINGS AND FIGURING OUT WHAT JOBS YOU'RE BEST AT.

BEING A HERO DEMANDS A NUMBER OF DIFFERENT QUALITIES.

LUXURY APT.

GRR!

IT'S EASY FOR KIDS LIKE YOU TO END UP AS HEROES WHO DON'T KNOW A THING ABOUT HOW SOCIETY REALLY WORKS.

YOU TWO, WITH YOUR BOMBASTIC QUIRKS, WILL PROBABLY END UP FIGHTING VILLAINS, MOSTLY.

...WILL HELP YOU BECOME HEROES WITH *DEPTH*.

HAVING A VARIETY OF EXPERIENCES NOW...

NO. 90!!

WE GOT A REQUEST TO DISPATCH TWO OF OUR FLEDGLINGS TO SOME SMALL-TOWN EVENT.

THEY SPECIFICALLY REQUESTED OUR MOST PROMISING YOUNG HEROES.

REPENTING FOR CRIMES

BAKUGO, TODOROKI. YOU'RE GOING. THIS IS A GOOD OPPORTUNITY.

HUH ?!

1ST PLACE AT SPORTS FESTIVAL

2ND PLACE

SCOUTED 3,556 TIMES POST-SPORTS FESTIVAL

SCOUTED 4,123 TIMES

75

DON'T TAG ME

THAT WAS INCREDIBLE. YOU'LL MAKE A FINE PAIR OF SUPER-HEROES SOMEDAY!

I SAW YOU TWO AT THE SPORTS FESTIVAL.

MAYOR

SO I'M SORRY ABOUT THE COSTUMES.

BA——BAM!!

SPEAK FOR YOURSELF!!

DON'TCHA GOT SOMETHING LESS CRINGE-WORTHY TO WEAR?!

BOM

NONSENSE. WE'RE READY TO WORK HARD.

NOT FOR THE REPUTA-TION I WANNA BUILD!!

WOMP

THE OTHER COSTUMES ARE EVEN MORE GIMMICKY.

THE KIDS TELL ME THEY'RE GREAT FOR SOCIAL MEDIA POSTING.

BIRD

CASE IN POINT

THIS IS DUMB.

KTUNK

KTUNK

YOU THINK SO?

...HAS A NICE RING TO IT.

I'M ACTUALLY GRATE-FUL, SINCE "A HERO WITH DEPTH"...

TCH.

WHAT-EVER. I JUST HATE DUMB SMALL-TOWN FESTIVALS!

BAD MEMORIES

GIVE JOBS LIKE THAT TO THE THIRD-RATE EXTRAS!

THAT'S WHY HE PICKED YOU.

...

I'M SURE SENSEI DOESN'T WANT YOU TO END UP A PRO WHO TREATS OTHER HEROES LIKE THEY'RE BENEATH YOU. LIKE YOU'RE DOING NOW.

76

EGG ON HIS FACE

AHEM.

THANK YOU FOR VISITING YOLKSVILLE, THE MOST "EGGS-CELLENT" TOWN IN THE TRI-PREFECTURE REGION.

BIRD

TAKE ONE

CHEW

CHEW

ARE THEY GOOD?

WHY HIS OWN FACE?

THESE ARE THE PASTRIES I MADE FOR THE FESTIVAL.

GO ON, BE HONEST.

...VERY... TASTY.

AND IF YOU'RE TRYING TO PUSH THE WHOLE EGG MOTIF... WHAT'S THE POINT IN USING YOUR FACE?

THE EGGY TEXTURE AIN'T COMING THROUGH ENOUGH... AND THERE'S NO AFTER-TASTE AT ALL.

BAKUGO!

HMPH.

I MEAN IT! KIDS THESE DAYS ARE SO SERIOUS, BUT THEY DON'T HAVE THE COURAGE TO SPEAK UP!

FAIR POINTS!! I APPRECIATE IT!

FWP

LOOK, YOU WANTED HONESTY.

LEAD BY EGGSAMPLE

IT'S WHY WE THROW EXTRA SUPPORT BEHIND YOU BABY HEROES.

SEE? ALL PART OF THE THEME.

IN THIS TOWN, WE PROMOTE OUR FAMOUS EGGS.

BIRD

FOR THE FINALE, YOU'LL DO THE CHICK DANCE UP ON STAGE.

THIS CAN'T END WELL.

OKAY.

AS MASCOTS, YOU'LL HAND OUT CHICK FANS AND ENGAGE WITH THE CHILDREN.

EGGS FEST

EGGS

W-WHY'RE YOU SO INTO THIS, HALF 'N' HALF?!

HUH?!

WHAT'S THE CHICK DANCE?

AH, I'LL TEACH YOU THE STEPS ON YOUR LUNCH BREAK.

!!

BAKUGO. WE'RE NOT AT SCHOOL, SO MIND YOUR DAMN MANNERS.

FLIPPING DAD THE BIRD

YOU'RE GREAT WITH THE KIDS, THOUGH. THEY LOVE YOU.

UGH! I CAN'T BELIEVE WHAT I PUT UP WITH!

NOM NOM

OH...? YOU DECIDED ON A COSTUME CHANGE AFTER ALL!!

BAM!!

SPLORT

CHICKEN OR EGG?

MR. MAYOR. TEACH ME THOSE DANCE STEPS, PLEASE.

THIS MAY BE A SMALL TOWN, BUT THERE WILL BE TV CAMERAS, YOU KNOW? ARE YOU SURE ABOUT THIS?

BAM

NEVER MIND THAT.

AREN'T YOU ENDEAVOR'S SON, THOUGH?

UGH. I CAN'T BELIEVE WHAT I PUT UP WITH!

YOU!! CONVINCE YOUR FRIEND, PLEASE!

We'll be sued!

IF I CAN DISGRACE MY FATHER'S NAME AT THE SAME TIME, THAT'S TWO BIRDS, ONE STONE.

I'M WORRIED ABOUT THE BLOWBACK ON ME!!

A FACE ONLY A MOTHER COULD—OH, WAIT...

YUM YUM!

MR. CHICK!

GET AWAY FROM ME! SCRAM!

YAY YAY

...TO PLAY WITH ME?

Would you like...

HEY.

ALONE

YO!! GET OFFA MY LEG!!

GLOMP

EEEK!! SCARY!!

SCARY...

STUMBLE

EASIER SAID THAN DONE.

H-HUHH?! ARE YOU CRYING?!

GRAH

GRAH

TODOROKI!! AT LEAST MAKE AN EFFORT!

"LOCAL PRODUCTION, FOR LOCAL CONSUMPTION..."

CHICKEN OR EGG?

"IF YOU WANNA FIND OUT, CHICKEN OR EGG—YOLKSVILLE'S THE PLACE, SO DON'T MAKE US BEG(G)!"

SOFT-BOILED PUNNY YOLKS

OH BOY, IT'S A REAL SCRAMBLE IN YOLKS-VILLE TODAY!

INDEED! I'M ENVIOUS THAT OUR CLASSMATES WERE SELECTED FOR THIS PREST-EGGIOUS EVENT!

I WANNA EAT SOME EGG BUNS.

BABAM

I WONDER WHERE THOSE TWO ARE AT...

WE CAN LOOK FOR 'EM WHILE EGGSPLORING AND EGGSAMINING THE STALLS.

WE OUGHT TO OBSERVE THEM AT WORK FOR FUTURE REFERENCE!

GLANCE

GLANCE

A SHELL-EBRATION? SOMEONE'S UP ON THAT STAGE!

COULD IT BE ...?

"SHELL-EBRA-TION"? PFFT.

BUZZ BUZZ

THE SCHEDULE SAYS IT'S A "CHICK DANCE" BY BABY HEROES FOR GOOD LUCK!

THOSE MUST BE OUR SCHOOL-MATES!

I'm eggstatic

UH... THEY SHOULD'VE GONE TO A HERO PRE-SCHOOL TO RECRUIT FOR THAT.

MURDER ON THE YOLKSVILLE EGGSPRESS

SHADDUP. WHAT'S DONE IS DONE.

I'M SORRY FOR GETTING YOU MORE INVOLVED...

KTUNK KTUNK

THAT HIT ME HARDER THAN I THOUGHT.

...WHEN SENSEI IMPLIED I WAS SOME SORT OF IGNORANT, IVORY TOWER ELITE.

I GUESS IT MADE ME A LITTLE ANGRY...

!!

SHP

ARE YOU... EVEN LISTENING?

...

DOOM DOOM DOOM

I-I SWEAR, WE DIDN'T *TRY* TO GET ON THE SAME RETURN TRAIN... AHHH!

BOOOM!

WHY'RE YOU THREE DWEEBS HERE?!

THE VICTIM: DEKU'S CAMERA

CARB THERAPY

I CAN'T BELIEVE HOW CRAZY THIS IS.

I'M BEGGING TO MAKE IT STOP!

"YOLKSVILLE'S THE PLACE, SO DON'T MAKE US BEG(G)!"

I WOULD THINK BAKUGO WOULD BE THE MORE RESISTANT OF THE TWO...

UNEGGSPECTED.

I-I'M KINDA SURPRISED TODOROKI AGREED TO THIS.

RIGHT...? KACCHAN HAS SOME EXPERIENCE, THOUGH...

WE SHALL GIVE IT OUR ALL!

Life is rough...

YUP. IT'S ALL A POPULARITY CONTEST IN THE END.

I GUESS THIS MEANS THOSE OF US WITH AVERAGE GRADES HAD BETTER PUT IN MORE EFFORT...

GLOOM

HUH?! THE IMPLICATION WAS THAT WE SHOULD RUSH HOME AND START TRAINING, THOUGH...?!

SIGH...

NOTHING LEFT TO DO BUT STUFF OUR FACES WITH EGG BUNS...

YEAH. BUT FOOD ALWAYS COMES FIRST.

STAIN IS GRATEFUL FOR *SMASH!!*

THE MAN WHO TURNED TO CRIME AND DIRTIED HIS HANDS WITH SIN.

STAIN

THE MAN WHO LOST FAITH IN MODERN HEROES AND TRIED TO CHANGE THE SYSTEM.

BUT THEY GAVE US THE MOST *DANGEROUS?!*

PSST PSST

HRM. I REQUESTED THAT THEY SEND US THEIR MOST DOCILE PRISONER.

IS IT SAFE TO HAVE HIM HERE?

IF YOU'RE SURE...

YOU MEAN IT?

ACTUALLY. AS LONG AS ALL MIGHT'S HERE, STAIN IS THE SAFEST VILLAIN TO TALK TO.

I'LL HELP IN ANY WAY I CAN...

SOB... MY GOD... ALL MIGHT... IN THE FLESH...

THOSE ARE TEAR-STAINS?

PLIP

PLIP

WANT TO KNOW MORE ABOUT VILLAINS?

THEN WHY NOT TALK TO ONE?

FSSH

ON THAT NOTE...

NO. 91!!

HUH...?

RMM

MM

WE HAVE A SPECIAL GUEST SPEAKER TODAY!!

ARE YOU KIDDING?!

SO BRIGHT... AHH.

MM

INDEED, KIDS... I WAS ALSO SHOCKED... THAT HE AGREED TO DO THIS.

MM

MM

BADDEST

I-I'M SO SORRY FOR STEPPING ON YOUR TOES!!

DON'T WORRY. IT'S FINE.

OH!

ERM... COULD I ASK YOU TO SPEAK MORE ABOUT THE MINDSET OF A VILLAIN?

SINCE I ALREADY TEACH THE KIDS ABOUT HERO STUFF...

I AM... THE ULTIMATE FORM OF EVIL.

HE SUCKS AT THIS!!

MWA HAH HAH...

THE VILLAIN MINDSET, RIGHT...

HM.

YOU WOULD COMPARE ME TO *STAIN*...?

MWA HAH HAH...

YEP!

HE'S AS BAD AS IDA.

OOPS.

GLOOM

SERIOUSLY?

TH-THAT'S NOT HOW I MEANT IT!

GAH!! WE MEAN YOU'RE BAD AT BEING BAD!

SORRY, IDA!

EAGER FOR APPROVAL

THEY SHOULD WELCOME BOTH PRAISE AND CRITICISM AS THEY WALK A LONELY, NOBLE PATH.

LISTEN UP. HEROES SHOULDN'T BE IN IT FOR THE COMPENSATION.

SURE, I'M WITH YOU SO FAR, BUDDY...

GLANCE

BEAM

HUH?

GLANCE

...GEEK. POWER ONLY IN PURSUIT OF YOUR IDEALS AND CONVICTIONS!!

SELF-SACRIFICE! NOT SELF-RIGHTEOUSNESS! WITH LOVE AND COURAGE IN YOUR HEARTS...

WHAT A NEEDY GUY...

PLIP

PLIP

MM-HMM, I CAN GET ON BOARD WITH ALL THAT.

SOB.

AHH...

KARMIC BALANCE

...IN ORDER TO SAVE MY PARENTS' COMPANY, WHICH IS FAILING. IS THAT BAD?

SOOO...I'M ACTUALLY HOPING TO BECOME A HERO...

SO BOLD, URARAKA.

HUH?! WHAT SOUND REASONING!

YOU CAN'T TURN TO OTHERS FOR THAT ANSWER. YOU NEED TO DECIDE FOR YOURSELF.

I THOUGHT SO. THANKS.

WHY SHOULD YOUR SAVING LIVES BE LINKED TO YOUR FAMILY'S COMPANY?

SIGH. BUT THERE'S SOMETHING WRONG WITH THE WORLD IF YOU'RE EVEN ASKING THAT QUESTION.

HUH?

IF HER PRIORITY IS THE COMPANY, THEN SHE WON'T PRIORITIZE HELPING PEOPLE AS A HERO...

JUST EXPEL HER.

I DOUBT THAT'S WHAT SHE MEANT...

STAIN'S THE DEBATE CHAMP!

YOU'RE... NOT WRONG...

SHP

ON SWITCH

ZOOM

EXCELLENT QUESTION, JIRO!

UM... SO WHAT WOULD YOU DO IF YOU FOUND A MILLION YEN ON THE GROUND?

*ABOUT $10,000

YOU GOODIE TWO-SHOES!!

BRING IT TO THE POLICE?

WHAT IF ENDEAVOR SHOWED UP RIGHT NOW?

WHAT IF MY DAD...

!!

THAT FRAUD...

HA! TO PURGE SOCIETY OF ITS FILTH...I WOULD HAVE TO SLIT HIS THROAT.

HUH?! THAT'S HIS TRIGGER? VILLAINS ARE SUPER SCARY!

DOOM

WHAT THE HECK?!

BA—M

QUIZ-A-VILLAIN

TRUE, BUT NOT MY POINT.

HUH?

B-BUT HAVING A STABLE INCOME WOULD ALLOW US TO FOCUS BETTER ON THE HERO WORK, NO?

Yeah!

SPENDING MONEY ON THIS, THOUGH? ISN'T THAT EXACTLY WHAT MAKES HIM MAD?

MAD? NO, I APPLAUD THIS.

TA-DA

YOU WERE SO ENTHUSIASTIC ABOUT THE Q&A THAT I THOUGHT, "WHY NOT LITERALLY SET THE STAGE FOR IT?"

PEOPLE GIVE DONATIONS TO MONKS AFTER A FUNERAL, BUT WOULD THOSE SAME MONKS SAY, "I HAVE NO MONEY, SO I REFUSE TO READ THE RITES FOR YOUR LOVED ONE"?

YOUR LOGIC IS FLAWED TO START WITH.

THEY CREATE JOBS IN THE COMMUNITY, AND ONCE THEY RECOUP COSTS, ANY ADDITIONAL PROCEEDS GO DIRECTLY TO THOSE IN NEED.

GLANCE
GLANCE

I RECOGNIZE THIS EQUIPMENT. IT COMES FROM ONE OF ALL MIGHT'S NON-PROFITS.

IT'S THAT CYNICAL SIDE OF SOCIETY THAT I REALLY HATE.

HMM... YEAH, THAT MAKES SENSE.

SAME THING WITH HEROES. YOU CAN'T PUT A PRICE TAG ON PEOPLE'S LIVES.

YES, BUT IT'S A LITTLE SCARY HOW KNOWLEDGE-ABLE HE IS.

I KNEW ALL THAT TOO!!

SHAKA

WOW.

UM, IS THAT TRUE?

NEVER FORGET. ALL MIGHT IS A SUPER-HERO IN EVERY SENSE OF THE WORD.

SUCH A PURE, NAIVE QUESTION.

ALL MIGHT...

SO WHY DIDJA DO ALL THOSE BAD AND MEAN THINGS, MISTER?

LESSON PLAN GONE AWRY

I HATE GEMS... SIGH.

YOUR FAVORITE GEM?

GO, GO, WIDDLE MIGHT.

A KIDS' CARTOON!

UMM... FAVORITE TV SHOW?

DING DING

LESSON PLANNING SURE IS TOUGH!

Favorite food?

Favorite color?

EVERYTHING WAS GOING GREAT, SO I THOUGHT THE WHOLE GAMESHOW DEAL WOULD TURN IT INTO A FULL-FLEDGED DISCUSSION, YET...

OR THOUGHTS ABOUT ME, GIVEN THAT YOU'RE A VILLAIN...?

AHEM. DO YOU HAVE ANY QUESTIONS FOR ME?

I'VE GOT TO GET THEM BACK ON TRACK.

QUIZ-A-VILLAIN

!!

HUH? IT WAS ANGUS STEAK.

DING DING

OH... UM... WHAT'D YOU HAVE FOR DINNER LAST NIGHT...?

STAIN WENT BACK TO PRISON EXTRA FULFILLED.

PROFILING

I WAS CONVINCED THAT WAS THE ONLY WAY I COULD EVER CHANGE THE SYSTEM.

NEXT.

SO, TURNING BACK THE CLOCK... WHY DID YOU DO...WHAT YOU DID...?

A-ASHIDO! GOING FOR THE JUGULAR!

ME, ME!

DO YOU HAVE ANY FRIENDS?

DING DING

AWW!!

I DO NOT.

NEXT.

CREEPY!

SIGH. THAT KNOBBY ANKLE BONE. NEXT.

GEEZ, MINETA !!

FAVORITE PART OF A WOMAN'S BODY?

BEST JEANIST

THE NO. 4 HERO AND SUPERSTAR OF THE FASHION WORLD!! HE'S ALSO THE SORT OF WEIRDO—I MEAN SUPERSTAR, WHO SIMPLY LIVES FOR TYING UP KACCHAN!!

HE'S NEVER QUITE SURE HOW TO BEST INTERACT WITH PEOPLE, SO HE USUALLY JUST COMES OFF AS A STRICT DISCIPLINARIAN. BUT MUTUAL UNDERSTANDING BETWEEN HIM AND OTHERS WOULD PROBABLY MEAN FEWER EMBARRASSING PUNISHMENTS ALL AROUND... MAYBE?!

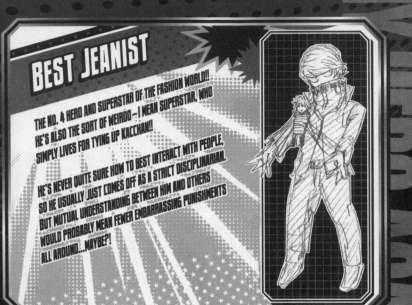

PRESENT MIC

VALUABLE AMONG THE DUDE CHARACTERS, SINCE HE LIVES HIS LIFE FREE AND UNCONSTRAINED BY THE EXPECTATIONS OF OTHERS!!

HE TAKES A BEATING AND KEEPS ON TICKING, WHICH IS APPARENTLY INSPIRING TO A LOT OF READERS OUT THERE?!

THAT SAID, HE CLEARLY DOESN'T VALUE HIS OWN LIFE VERY MUCH, GIVEN HOW UNAFRAID HE IS TO ANTAGONIZE HIS SURLY FORMER CLASSMATE, AIZAWA!!

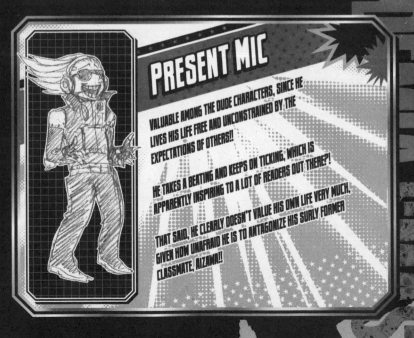

JEKYLLED

HIS WORDS AND BEHAVIOR MAY SEEM ODD, BUT IT HAD THE EFFECT OF REFORMING HIM, MOSTLY.

THE VILLAIN'S QUIRK WAS *GOODFACE*, AND WELL, YOU CAN SEE WHAT IT DID.

Enough pointless prattle, Sensei...

SMAK

Why don't we start the lesson?

ARGH! SOMEBODY FIX ME!!

GAH

NOT WHAT I MEANT !!

AS YOU CAN SEE...

OUR LITTLE TOUGH GUY IS SO DEDICATED!

IN THE MEANTIME, I EXPECT FULL COOPERATION.

...BUT HE DIDN'T WANT TO FALL BEHIND ON HIS STUDIES, SO HERE HE IS.

...I RECOMMENDED THAT HE STAY HOME UNTIL THE EFFECTS FADE...

NO. 92!!

I HAVE A SPECIAL ANNOUNCEMENT TODAY.

BAKUGO ENCOUNTERED A VILLAIN...AND IS STILL FEELING THE EFFECTS.

YOU'VE BEEN WARNED.

WHAT?

BAM !!

WHO IS THAT?!

THE ADVENTURES OF BAKUGO: HANG IN THERE, KACCHAN

WHY THIRTEEN IS HER FAVORITE

DIAMOND DUST?!

Translation: "Damn it!"

DIAMOND DUST!!

PFFT.

S-SORRY! BUT, "FLY AWAY"? REALLY?

The full moon ought not laugh before the blazing sun! Fly away!

GASP

GLARE

VA M

WAIT. WHY'D HE CALL ME *FULL MOON*...? OH.

ROUND-FACE

NOT ESPECIALLY? IT'S CUTE.

HEY. IS MY FACE REALLY THAT ROUND?

KATSUN BAKUDERE

Might just be that way. What of it?

FWP

BUT WHEN IT WEARS OFF, HE'S BACK TO HIS ROTTEN SELF?

SO HE HAS THESE SPASMS WHERE HE ACTS EXTRA SUAVE FOR A BIT?

It can only lead to heartbreak.

HE'S LIKE A PARODY.

It's best you pay me no mind at all!

"WHEREVER YOU ARE, THAT'S WHERE I FIND MY HAPPINESS!!"

GAH HA HA HA HA!

AND THEN YOU SAID, "I'D GLADLY MARCH INTO HELL, IF IT WERE WITH YOU!"

EEK!! SORRY, MAN!!

HOW 'BOUT I CARVE THAT LESSON ONTO YOUR FRONTAL LOBES?

FWP

DIDN'TCHA HEAR SENSEI'S WARNING? HE TOLDJA TO LEAVE ME BE...

88

THE HEARTS OF MEN

LOW-CUT V-NECK

TOTAL KNOCKOUT

HERO

You'll never lay a finger on me at that speed.

Your attacks appear frozen in place to me.

BAM

VILLAIN

ZASH

You're going to be okay, kiddo.

I hope you're not... hurt...

OH?

GACK!

HOSTAGE

KRAK

ARGH!!

URK!

PENDULUM BACKBREAKER

TWITCH

SENSE!!! MIDORIYA'S DEAD!!

Smooth transition though...

GO FETCH RECOVERY GIRL!!

FROM A DAMSEL-CARRY INTO A BACK-BREAKER. THAT ONE'S GOTTA HURT...

A REAL ROMEO

SPARKL

Hey there...

Y-YES?

HOSTAGE

VILLAIN

Accept that you're going to be mine.

Just give in already.

HUH?!

SMAK

We can dine in hell. Together.

How about a date?

HUH?!

EEEK

HE SAID SOMETHING ABOUT DINING IN HELL AND THEN BLEW HIMSELF UP...

IT'S NOT WHAT IT LOOKS LIKE!

WHOA! WHAT'D YOU DO TO HIM?

OH... I THINK I GET IT.

HERO

90

IDOL CULTURE

OVER HERE, KATSUKI!

KATSUKI!!

YAP YAP

GAB GAB

WORD GOT AROUND, AND NOW HE'S GOT HIS OWN FAN CLUB.

FOR REAL?!

My little Katsudon!!

Prince Katsuki!!

Sweet Baku-Baby!!

UM... WHAT'S ALL THIS?

I shall never love another woman again.

BE GONE.

SQUEE!!

FWP

I'm sorry, ladies. But I vowed to dedicate myself to pursuing my dreams.

REALLY?!

IT ALMOST SEEMS LIKE THEY'RE INTO THAT SWITCH BETWEEN CHARMING AND FURIOUS...

IT TOOK A WHILE FOR THE EXCITEMENT TO DIE DOWN...

SQUEE!

GAH!! QUIT YAPPING AND GET THE HELL OUTTA MY FACE!!

INNER TURMOIL

I SHOULD'VE STAYED HOME AFTER ALL...

GU home.

UGH! THIS'S WIPING ME OUT.

WORMP

NOT WHEN I'M THE ONE WHO ALWAYS NEEDS SAVING!

GLARE

NO! WHO CARES IF I'M IMPOSING ON THE REST OF THESE LOSERS!

I... I...

I NEED TO GET STRONGER.

TMP TMP

I'VE JUST GOT... SO MANY FEEL-INGS INSIDE.

GRP

B-BAKUGO?

AAM

Until I can show them how I shine brighter than any other!!

META TWIST

IT'S MAY 1?! WHEN'D WE ENTER THE NEW YEAR?!

WE'LL DO THE SHOW, BUT THIS IS ABOUT SOMETHING ELSE.

HUH...? YOU KIDS DON'T WANT TO DO IT?

B!! AM MAY 1 11:05

I REMEMBER THINKING THIS LAST TIME TOO, THAT SOMETHING STRANGE WAS GOING ON...

Yeah!! Sounds like fun!!

Last year?

THIS IS DEFINITELY THE THIRD ONE OF THESE SHOWS WE'RE DOING...

STRANGE? HOW SO?

THAT'D MEAN THAT WE WERE HELD BACK TWO GRADES.

GOLDEN WEEK (THIS YEAR)

GOLDEN WEEK (LAST YEAR)

GOLDEN WEEK (TWO YEARS AGO)

IT'S LIKE...IF THIS IS OUR THIRD SHOW, THEN AT LEAST TWO YEARS HAVE GONE BY.

ACK!!

THIS IS MORE THAN YOU JUST GOING SENILE!!

Y-YOU'RE RIGHT!! PARDON ME! I'M LOSING MY SENSE OF TIME IN MY OLD AGE...

ATTENTION, KIDS!! IT'S TIME FOR THE ANNUAL GOLDEN WEEK HERO SHOW!!

YOU'LL DO IT, RIGHT?! SAY IT WITH ME!!

NO. 93!!

UH, HANG ON... DID HE SAY GOLDEN WEEK?!

OKAY!

...US ...RA!

ISN'T IT ACTUALLY HALLOWEEN ...?

BAM

P-PRETTY BOLD OF YOU TO WALTZ IN HERE!!

THE LEAGUE OF VILLAINS?! GASP!!

YOU SHOULD BE ROLLING OUT THE RED CARPET.

...THE REASON YOU SNOT-NOSED IDIOTS CAN'T MOVE UP A GRADE.

BECAUSE WE HAPPENED TO BRING WITH US...

?!

SO WE CONDUCTED OUR OWN INVESTIGATION.

YOU SEE, WE SENSED THERE WAS A REASON TIME WASN'T PROGRESSING.

IT'S RESPONSIBLE FOR LOCKING US DOWN WITHIN THE SPACE-TIME CONTINUUM.

AND WE FIGURED OUT THAT IT'S CUZ OF THIS GUY'S QUIRK— ISEKAI.

HUH?!

TIME

NOOO... I TOTALLY *AM* THE TYPE TO GET HELD BACK IN SCHOOL!

SILENT

DID ALL OF YOU REALIZE THIS?

GAH! SAME HERE!

THEY BARELY SAVED UP MY TUITION FOR ALL THREE YEARS...

H-HOW DO I EXPLAIN THIS TO MOM AND DAD...?

URARAKA HAS GONE ALL FROTHY!!

BURBL!

BURBL!

WHEN DID THAT HAPPEN...?

MUTTER

WHO CARRIES AROUND PILES OF OLD DIARIES?!

IT'S TRUE... I HAVE OVER 700 DIARY ENTRIES SINCE SCHOOL BEGAN!!

MUTTER MUTTER MUTTER

WE NEED TO HAVE A TALK ABOUT THIS...

PERFECT TIMING, IT LOOKS LIKE.

?!

ZRM ZRM ZRM ZRM

FORESHADOWING

RIGHT. LET'S GO OVER WHAT WE KNOW.

THIS IS TOO MUCH PLOT. MY BRAIN CAN'T KEEP UP.

1-A

BUZZ

BUZZ BUZZ

FIRST...

COME TO MENTION IT, I REMEMBER CELEBRATING NEW YEAR'S TWICE.

THAT'S LIKE, CRAZY.

YEAH!!

AT SOME POINT, WE GOT THROWN INTO A WORLD WHERE THE SEASONS CHANGE, BUT TIME DOESN'T ACTUALLY PASS.

RIGHT... LIKE SAZAE-SAN, OR THE SIMPSONS, OR OTHER CARTOONS.

THOSE ARE HIGH-PROFILE REFERENCES!!

Big sis!

Darn you, Katsuo!

YOU SAID YOU'LL SEND US BACK ONCE YOU SEE OUR SHOW... BUT WE HAVEN'T BEEN AGING, RIGHT?

YOU'RE A SHARP ONE. YES, THE VALENTINE'S DAY EVENT WAS THE FIRST ONE REMOVED FROM TIME.

THERE WERE MORE AND MORE, AFTER THAT.

THE BIG CHANGE HAPPENED RIGHT AFTER OUR TRAINING CAMP, RIGHT?

GROUNDHOG YEAR

WUZZAT MEAN? I'M LOST-ER THAN LOST.

SIZZLE

THIS SERIES ISN'T SUPPOSED TO BE SCI-FI.

WHAT THE! THIS ISN'T A SCI-FI SERIES!!

THAT'S WHAT I SAID.

SPRING
SUMMER
WINTER
FALL

I GUESS THAT GUY'S QUIRK THREW US INTO A DIMENSION WHERE WE CAN'T ADVANCE TO THE NEXT YEAR?

WE TRIED THREATENING HIM, TO MAKE HIM SEND US BACK TO OUR WORLD...

YES.

C'MON, YOU GOTTA UNDO THIS!

I NEED TO GRADUATE HIGH SCHOOL!

...WE GIVE HIM THE GREATEST HERO SHOW OF ALL TIME.

FOR REAL?!

...BUT HE ABSO-LUTELY REFUSES TO DO SO UNLESS...

NOD NOD

BIRTH OF A VILLAIN

HOWEVER...

IT WAS LIKE YOU KIDS MONOPO- LIZED HIM.

MEGA YUKS

ONCE HE STARTED WORKING AT U.A. HE WASN'T EVERYONE'S «HERO» ANYMORE.

...I THOUGHT...

WHICH IS WHY...

GOOSH

...I COULD JUST TAKE ALL MIGHT...

SAD BACKSTORY

WELL ...

YEAH! WHY?!

BUT WHY?

...I'M JEALOUS OF YOU KIDS.

?!

IT'S BECAUSE ...

ONLY ABLE TO VIEW YOUR WORLD AS IF THROUGH A TV SCREEN...

BECAUSE OF THIS QUIRK OF MINE, I'VE BEEN HERE IN MY OWN DIMENSION ALL ALONE, ALL MY LIFE.

I WANTED TO MEET HIM, BUT HE'S EVERYONE'S HERO, SO I WAS SATISFIED JUST WATCHING FROM A DISTANCE....

FWP

I LOVED ALL MIGHT MORE THAN ANYTHING, THOUGH. THE ULTIMATE SUPER- HERO, WHO ALWAYS SAVES THE DAY WITH A SMILE.

A MULTI-CHAPTER ARC?!

...SO IT SEEMED WISE NOT TO DO ANYTHING THAT COULDN'T BE UNDONE.

WE HAD NO ASSURANCE THAT WOULD WORK...

...KURO-GIRI?

WHAT WAS THE POINT OF THIS...

CHF CHF

YOU CAN'T BEAT ME LIKE THAT.

I'M THE MASTER OF THIS DIMENSION, OKAY?

I'LL PLAY THE PART OF THE VILLAIN...

...AND I WANT TO SEE MORE THAN JUST PROS THERE.

I'M LOOKING FORWARD TO THE HERO SHOW.

I APPRECIATE YOUR COOPERATION.

BOW

ALL OF YOU, COMBINE YOUR STRENGTH TO BRING ME DOWN, PLEASE.

TO BE CONTINUED

PROBLEM SOLVED

...EVEN THOUGH I KNEW HOW WRONG IT WAS.

I TRIED TO KEEP UP THE PRETENSE BY ENFORCING SOME FORM OF CONTINUITY...

BUT I AM PREPARED TO *END IT ALL.*

!!

AS LONG AS I LIVE...THIS DIMENSION WILL EXIST.

...I JUST WANTED...

...TO GO OUT IN AS DRAMATIC A WAY AS POSSIBLE.

I KNOW MY REQUEST MIGHT SEEM SELFISH, YET...

I KNEW KILLING HIM WAS THE RIGHT MOVE.

OH NO!!

GRP

HERE YA GO.

96

LET THE SHOW BEGIN

... ...

WE DON'T HAVE A CHOICE, DO WE?

UGH. IS THIS REALLY GONNA WORK?

IT IS TIME...

ZOOOM

?!

SHALL WE?

I'M GRATEFUL THAT YOU'VE TAKEN MY REQUEST SERIOUSLY.

NO. 94!!

AT SOME POINT, WE GOT TRAPPED IN A DIMEN-SION WHERE YEARS DON'T PASS AT ALL...

...AND THE ONLY WAY TO ESCAPE IS BY BEATING THE MASTER OF THIS DIMENSION.

AFTER A LONG DISCUS-SION...

...WE DECIDED ON JUST THE HERO SHOW TO MAKE THAT HAPPEN.

97

GENRE MASHUP

H-HE TRANS-FORMED...

W-WELL, WE'VE COME THIS FAR RELYING ON DUMB JOKES AND GAGS, SO WHY QUIT NOW?!

MY ERASURE CLEARLY DOESN'T WORK.

SEE?! THAT GUY'S REALLY TAKING THIS SERIOUSLY!!

EEK SO SCARY! TEE HEE.

BAN

O-OH NO. LOOK. A VILLAIN.

LET'S GIVE HIM A HERO SHOW, OUR WAY!!

C

B

VILLAGER A

SO MANY VILLAGER EXTRAS!

G

H

D

I

J

F

E

M

L

K

PLEASE DON'T DESTROY OUR MEDIEVAL VILLAGE...?

THE CURTAIN RISES...

BA

...ON OUR FINAL HERO SHOW!!

SPACE-TIME VILLAIN: ISEKAI

HE'S GOT THE WHOLE WORLD IN HIS HANDS!

PREPARE YOURSELVES, BECAUSE...

I WON'T GO DOWN WITHOUT A FIGHT.

WHO LET SHIGARAKI CRAFT ANYTHING?

MEANIE! YOU TOOK EVERYTHING FROM US!

BIG VIN

LEAP

HUH?

I'M SORRY, I DIDN'T KNOW! WAIT—THAT'S YOUR VILLAGE?!

STAGECRAFT

THAT'S ASKING A LOT.

VILLAGE

JUST IMAGINE THAT PIECE OF PAPER IS THE VILLAGE!

IMAGINATION...?

MR. ISEKAI! PUT YOUR IMAGINATION TO GOOD USE!

OH NO... MY BEAUTIFUL HOMETOWN, GONE, JUST LIKE THAT...

SHAKA

SHAKA

NOBLE PRINCE

TMP

...SHALL PAY FOR YOUR SINS!!

YOU...

GRP

PRINCE!!

HUH?!

1-A'S WAY

OH NO!! HE'S NOT PLAYING ALONG AT ALL!!

FLINCH

HUH... A MEDIEVAL VILLAGE?

GIVE AN AMATEUR THESPIAN A SCRIPT? THAT'S JUST SHOOTING YOURSELF IN THE FOOT.

WHAT EXACTLY ARE YOUR THEATER CREDENTIALS?!

KEY GRIP

SEE? I TOLD YOU WE SHOULD'VE GIVEN HIM THE SCRIPT IN ADVANCE.

DIRECTOR

NO NEED TO GET FANCY. JUST SAY WHAT'S ON YOUR MIND.

Director

OH.

MR. ISEKAI, JUST IMPROVISE! SAY WHAT COMES NATURALLY TO YOU!!

Director

BRAM

VILLAGE

HUH?

Y-YOU JUST DESTROYED IT, YOU JERK!

OH NO! I STEPPED ON THEIR VILLAGE.

UM... WHERE'S YOUR VILLAGE, EXACTLY?

what's on his mind

99

THE *SMASH!!* PERSPECTIVE

FOUL VILLAIN!!

VSH

PREPARE TO TASTE DEFEAT!!

UM...

RAH

WAIT...

WHOA!

RAH

GOONS A AND B

BAM

WE'RE HERE TO FIGHT FOR *YOU,* ISEKAI!!

TH-THEY'RE INSANE!!

BARBARIAN PRINCE

THE ROYAL ARMY FIGHTING THE BARBARIANS, AMIDST THE RUINS OF A VILLAGE! A WHOLE FANTASY WORLD!

RAH

RAH

I CAN SEE IT NOW!!

WHEN I WATCHED THEM FROM THE SHADOWS, IT ALWAYS SEEMED LIKE THE DUMBEST SORT OF NONSENSE.

WHAT'S THIS NOW?

RAH

IS THIS HOW THE WORLD LOOKS ALL THE TIME... THROUGH THEIR EYES...?

SHOTO'S SOLDIERS A-J

I AM HERE, AS BACKUP!!

ERM, "SHOTO, USE MY ARMIES TO FIGHT THAT FIEND."

KING OF AN ALLIED KINGDOM

THE PRINCE'S FATHER

SCRIPT

IN THE NAME OF OUR KING!!

WE FIGHT THE GOOD FIGHT!!

ALLIED SOLDIERS A-N

I'VE FOUND IT. A WAY TO RETURN YOU TO YOUR DIMENSION WITHOUT ME HAVING TO DIE...

SHALL I TRY IT OUT?!

BUT I'VE GROWN SO FOND OF YOU ALL.

OF COURSE I DON'T WANT TO DIE.

!!

SO I'LL ATONE FOR MY SINS, AND MAYBE SOMEDAY...

...WE CAN BE FRIENDS FOR REAL?

LOVE, HOPE, IMAGINATION, ETC.

IT MADE ME WONDER. I WANTED TO KNOW MORE.

THEIR MERRY-MAKING ALWAYS SEEMED LIKE SO MUCH FUN.

TIME

I THINK I GET IT NOW.

VILLAGE

THAT MIGHT JUST MAKE IT POSSIBLE TO...

WHAT I LACKED WAS IMAGINATION.

?!

VWOOM

FW

WHAT THE?!

AH

WH...

THE GREAT RESET

...TO MEET ALL OF YOU.

I'M SO VERY GLAD I GOT THE CHANCE...

...WHEN THAT DAY COMES, CHALLENGE ME AGAIN!!

ALL I ASK IS...

!!

YOU GOT IT!

THANK YOU!!

QUIRK: ISEKAI

IMAGINATION TRIUMPHS OVER ALL!!

Z R R R

OH, DEKU.

UM, DOES IT EVEN MAKE SENSE FOR THINGS TO BE BACK TO NORMAL AT THIS POINT?

AH!! URARA-WHAAA!

R-RECOVERY GIRL?! BUT WHY?!

GRAND SURPRISE

YOU'RE ACTING AS FIDGETY AS EVER, I SEE.

SMASH!! FROM HERE TO FOREVER

IS THIS OUR ORIGINAL DIMENSION?! IT CAN'T BE...!

WHAT, IS, HAPPENING ?!

OR IS THIS JUST HOW EVERY-ONE IS NOW THAT TWO YEARS HAVE REALLY PASSED?!

HEY.

SHAKA SHAKA

J-JUST CALM DOWN AND THINK!! WAIT. MAYBE THAT ISEKAI GUY FAILED?!

Ha ha ha. Better get a move on, friend.

PHEW. IT'S JUST KACCHAN AND...

SPARKL

What's got you acting so odd, Midoriya?

Don't be late to class!

DUH-DOOM

ACK! NO!! HOW'S THIS POSSIBLE ?!

FINAL CHAPTER (?) / END

NO. 2001, A SMASH!! ODYSSEY

HA HA HA, MIDORIYA! TRYING TO FLIRT WITH OUR FRIEND?!

THAT'S NOT HOW I... IDA?!

SHAKA SHAKA SHAKA

SO FORMAL. JUST CALL ME CHIYO.

REALLY? C-CAN I CARRY YOUR BAG FOR YOU?

YAOYOROZU! YOU MUSTN'T COME TO SCHOOL IN YOUR COSTUME!!

BUT CHANGING OUTTA IT IS SUCH A DRAG.

FWEE FWEE

UGH, SCHOOL IS SUCH A TOTAL DRAG.

WHO'S THAT ?!

YES, PAPA !!

PAPA ?!

BEEP BEEP

DON'T FORGET YOUR LUNCH NOW, SHOTO.

YOU'RE SO SILLY, PAPA!

DASH

GAH HA HA HA!!

SHOTO!! YOU FORGOT TO LET PAPA GIVE YOU A KISS. ♡

KISSY

!

LIKELIEST FANBOY

THIS MIGHT GET A LITTLE AWKWARD.

SEE YA!!

HE ALREADY DID IT!!

CATERING TO FANS, HUH?

BADUM BADUM

THE OTHER IS FINDING CREATIVE WAYS TO KEEP IT FROM INTERFERING WITH THE JOB!!

We judge EFFECTIVE SHILLING ON TWO POINTS!! ONE IS HOW EFFECTIVELY YOU KEEP THOSE HOPES AND DREAMS ALIVE FOR THE FANS.

End of the line, villain!!

FWP

HEY, WAIT A SECOND !!

THE SUPPORT COURSE WHIPPED UP THESE FAN ROBOTS, WHICH WILL GIVE YOU FEEDBACK ON THEIR SATISFACTION RATE!!

BAM

I HEARD THEY TOOK A SURVEY TO CREATE A COMPOSITE OF THE AVERAGE FAN, AND, WELL...

UGH!

WHY'RE THEY MODELED AFTER ME?!

HUH?!

AUTOGRAPH PLEASE.

GOOFING OFF IN SHONEN JUMP!! ①

A HERO IS A PERSON WHO CARRIES EVERYONE'S HOPES AND DREAMS!!

YOU NEED TO BE SKILLED AT CATERING TO FANS!!

THAT'S WHAT YOU'LL LEARN ABOUT TODAY!!

LEAP

ALL RIGHT FOR IZUKU

ALL RIGHT FOR IZUKU

ALL MIGHT'S DOING GREAT, EVEN IN THE **SMASH!!** DIMENSION!! HERE'S TO ANOTHER WONDERFUL (?) DAY OF TRAINING!!

SHOWING THEM AN ICE TIME

AUTOGRAPH PLEASE.

TMP TMP

A HERO.

LEAP

KSHK

SORRY, BUT I'M SHORT ON TIME.

HERE'S A SIGNATURE.

SPARKL

KRK

KRK KRK

WOW! A DYNAMIC SIGNATURE MADE OF ICE FRAGMENTS!!

THINK HOW I FEEL ABOUT IT!!

WHAT A SCENE.

SPLORT

TRUE TO LIFE

NOW, START!!

IN ORDER TO PASS, YOU HAVE TO SATISFY FIVE ROBO-FANS AND MAKE IT TO THE EMERGENCY SITE WITHIN ONE MINUTE!

PLEASE. AUTOGRAPH PLEASE.

CROWD CROWD

WOW. A HERO.

THIS IS KINDA CREEPY...

SHDDR

STARE

I HAVEN'T PRACTICED MY SIGNATURE...

I HOPE THIS IS GOOD ENOUGH.

EARPHONE JACK

A SATISFIED ROBOT WILL EXPERIENCE A WICKED NOSEBLEED!!

BUT WHY?!

SPLORT

INAUTHENTIC

...WHAT I CAN DO IS PREPARE AUTO-GRAPHS IN ADVANCE!!

I CAN'T PRODUCE A SPECTACLE LIKE TODOROKI, BUT...

LEAP

CREATY

ZRM ZRM ZRM

CREATION

THERE'S ONE FOR EVERY-ONE.

AUTOGRAPH PLEASE.

ME TOO, ME TOO.

CREATY

SHP SHP SHP SHP

NOT WRITTEN WITH TRUE FEELING.

THIS IS MASS-PRODUCED.

SNAP

THEY'RE GRUMPY!!

BUT, BUT...

PZZT

YOU SUCK, YOU KNOW THAT?

OH NO. I'M SORRY.

PERFECT AS FRISBEES, THOUGH.

FLING

THEY'RE NOT ME!! I'M WAY MORE POLITE!!

ALTERNATE WIN CONDITION

CANNOT WAIT.

AUTOGRAPH PLEASE.

Y-YIKES.

UM.

IT'S DEKU!!

BUT YOU'LL FLOAT AWAY.

HANDSHAKE PLEASE, MISS!!

BACK OFF!!

COME ON.

TWITCH

TWITCH

VICARIOUS SHOCK

OOF.

WHAM

I SAID, BACK OFF!! NO TOUCH-ING!!

SERIOUSLY?! GETTING YOUR BUTT KICKED WAS *SATISFYING*?!

SPLORT

OH HO HO... THANK YOU.

HAPPY ACCIDENT

YOU ROCK. I'M YOUR BIGGEST FAN.

AUTO-GRAPH.

GRR GRR

SHADDUP ALREADY!! THOSE FACES JUST PISS ME OFF!!

OUCH !!

SAY HI.

IT WON'T HURT.

BOO

OH? COOL.

NOT "COOL" !!

OW. OWW.

I-IT'S ME. I'M THE REAL ONE!

SHOOM

YEAH, CUZ HE BROKE MY FACE.

GAH, I'VE HAD ENOUGH!!

GUSH GUSH

PFFT.

PFFT. BLOODY NOSE? GUESS HE'S *SATISFIED*.

FAN TERMINATOR

I APPRECIATE THE SUPPORT !!

ZOOM

THANK YOU KINDLY!!

ZOOM

ZOOM

BUT THAT SPEED COULD BACK-FIRE.

LOOKIT ALL THAT BLOOD.

RIBBIT

OF COURSE IDA PRIORITIZES SPEED AND MANNERS ...

I CAN SATISFY EVERY LAST AUTOMATON AND REACH THE SCENE IN TIME.

HMPH !!

MY QUIRK MAKES THIS POSSIBLE!!

KZZT

KZZT

WAHHHH!!

TRUE TO LIFE, PART 2

...I WILL TEACH BY EXAMPLE.

TO FINISH OFF THIS EXERCISE...

BAM

HE... ALREADY DID IT!!

WOW. IT'S ALL MIGHT.

DOOT DOOT DOOT DOOT

ALL RIGHT

TURN

TMP

HOW, YOU ASK?

TOO COOL.

SPLORT

WAIT, NO! THIS IS DIFFERENT!!

SEE? NOSE-BLEED.

BECAUSE I WAS THERE.

5% OF AN AUTOGRAPH

SHOW US HOW IT'S REALLY DONE.

HOPES AND DREAMS, RIGHT.

YAP YAP

HERE WE GO! THE MAN OF THE HOUR!!

WAH WAH

SO LEMME TEST OUT ALL THAT TRAINING I'VE DONE!!

I'M AIMING TO BE JUST LIKE ALL MIGHT!!

ZOOM

FIVE PERCENT!!

ZOOM

ZOOM

ZOOM

ONE FOR ALL.

PLEASE.

AUTOGRAPH PLEASE.

ZOOM

DARN IT!! HOW DOES ALL MIGHT PULL THAT OFF?!

BA

M

HE ALREADY... WAIT, NO HE DIDN'T!!

GASP

AUTOGR—

108

VILLAIN ISLAND

OOH, THE SEA!! SO BLUE!!

SPLASH

HEY... YOU SAID THERE'S WORK TO BE DONE, SO I'M HERE.

Just woke up

ZRM ZRM ZRM

OH HO HO!! INDEED, THERE IS WORK.

WAIT. WHERE ARE WE?

WE'RE ALL GOING TO *WORK*...

...TO SURVIVE ON THIS UNINHABITED ISLAND!

VILLAIN ISLAND!!
PRODUCED BY KUROGIRI

BAM

HUH ?!

W-WHY ...?

SHARING RESOURCES AND COOPERATING SHOULD HELP BRING US TOGETHER.

YAY!

WHAT WE LACK IS GOOD TEAMWORK.

THE LEAGUE OF VILLAINS IS A GANG OF VICIOUS CRIMINALS.

BUT THESE SCOUNDRELS ARE SHORT ON A SENSE OF SOLIDARITY.

LAZE

LAZE

YES, THE TOKIO MEMBERS WERE SENT TO AN UNINHABITED ISLAND AND FORCED TO COOPERATE TO SURVIVE.

BAM

MIGHTY MIGHTY JUMP!!

JUMP ISLAND

BUILDING AN ENTIRE HOUSE FROM SCRATCH ?!

TH-THAT'S IT!!

VERY COOL.

WORK ETHICS

AND WITH A FRIDGE, WE COULD USE SEAWATER...

SURPRISINGLY INTO IT

DRINKING WATER, RIGHT. WELL, I'VE GOT SOME COCONUTS.

SHF

I BET THIS TINY ISLAND GETS PLENTY OF RAIN.

THERE'S LOTS OF LITTLE POOLS OF WATER.

MAYBE CUT DOWN SOME TREES TO CREATE HOLLOWED-OUT CONTAINERS.

WE OUGHTA MAKE SOMETHING TO COLLECT RAIN-WATER.

DASH

SHIGARAKI... AGAIN, YOU'RE MISSING THE POINT.

MEAN-WHILE

I USE *ALL* RESOURCES AVAILABLE TO ME. THAT'S MY STYLE.

MUTINY

MAKING FEWER MOUTHS TO FEED.

GRR

NOW THEN! WHAT'S THE MOST ESSENTIAL THING FOR SURVIVAL?

EXACTLY! WAIT, WHAT...?

HA HA, VERY CLEVER, BUT LET'S BE SERIOUS!

THE ANSWER IS, "SECURING A SOURCE OF DRINKING WATER."

WHY MAKE THIS DIFFICULT? THE GOAL IS TO ENGENDER TEAMWORK!

YEAH, WE'LL COOPERATE IN ORDER TO KILL YOU.

GINGER ALE'S JUST TASTIER WHEN YOU'RE OUT IN THE SUN.

PWAHH!

Ale

SOURCE OF DRINKS

QUIRK: WARP GATE

SHAKA SHAKA

YOU'RE MISSING THE POINT.

WARP ME IN SOME POTATO CHIPS TOO, KUROGIRI.

VACATION

IT ENDED UP BEING A PRETTY STANDARD SUMMER VACATION.

I GUESS THIS IS FINE.

MISSION STATEMENT

THIS AND THAT ARE TOTALLY DIFFERENT!

HUH?!

NOPE. SAME.

WHAT KIND OF FOOL FOLLOWS SOMEONE ELSE'S RULES BLINDLY...

...AND STILL CALLS HIMSELF A VILLAIN?

WE'RE TRYING TO DESTROY THE LAWS THAT KEEP US DOWN... AND WE JUST HAPPEN TO BE DOING IT TOGETHER.

WE'RE NOT OUT TO BUILD SOME NATION OF VILLAINS AND SING KUMBAYA.

TOUCHED IN THE HEAD, MAYBE! HE'S WRECKING YOUR WHOLE PLAN.

I'M TOUCHED.

SHIGARAKI... YOU'VE GROWN SO MUCH.

THESE GUYS ARE HOPELESS!!

WE SHALL SURVIVE HOWEVER WE SO CHOOSE, WHILE ENJOYING OURSELVES.

VERY WELL. NO MORE RESTRICTIONS FOR THIS EXCURSION.

GREAT. GLAD YOU'RE ON BOARD.

VOLUME 5 - END

THE BONUS CONTENT STARTS HERE!! AND FIRST UP IS THE ACTUAL FINAL CHAPTER OF SMASH!!, SO...

...GET READING!!

BONUS STUFF!!

MY HERO ACADEMIA SMASH

MODERN FAMILY

WAIT... WHAT? SATO?!

CH AK HUP

YOU'LL BE LATE FOR SCHOOL!

HUH?

SATO: IZUKU'S MOM

WHAT'S GOING ON?!

YOU STILL REFUSE TO CALL ME "MOMMY," HUH?

SAY WHAT?

BWUUUH?!

THANK YOU, MAMA MAGNE.

YOU MUSTN'T BE SO CRUEL TO MAMA SATO, ZU-KUN...

MAGNE: IZUKU'S MOM

WHAT THE HECK?! HOW DID THESE TWO PRODUCE ME?!

SMILES FOR ALL... THAT'S THE ONE RULE WE HAVE IN THIS HOUSEHOLD!

GUH HUH BUH ?!

FINAL CHAPTER!!

WITH OUR FINAL HERO SHOW OVER AND DONE WITH...

...WE FINALLY RETURNED TO OUR ORDINARY (?) EVERYDAY LIVES.

CHIRP

CHIRP

WAKE UP, IZUKU.

OR SO WE THOUGHT...

HRM...?

THE UPSIDE-DOWN

...YOU'LL BE DOING 2-ON-2 BATTLE TRAINING USING THE BUDDY SYSTEM.

UM, TODAY...

M-MOM?!

WAIT... BUT... THIS IS JUST...

UGH!

PLEASE DON'T CALL YOUR TEACHER "MOM."

HAR HAR, WHAT A DORK.

HA HA HA

YOU'VE BEEN ACTING SO WEIRD TODAY.

YIKES! ASHIDO?!

FIDGET

MIDORIYA!

THIS IS JUST TOO MUCH FOR ME TO HANDLE.

SHAKE IT UP, BABY!!

THERE'S CHIPPER, AND THEN THERE'S THIS!!

BAM

WHAT SHE SAID, MIDORIYA! WHERE'S YOUR USUAL CHIPPER SELF?!

SMASH!! CHAOS

GAB GAB

SO IT WASN'T JUST A DREAM...

...BUT THIS STILL FEELS PRETTY WARPED TO ME.

HE SAID HE'D GET US OUT OF THAT WARPED DIMENSION...

MRRR

YOU...IT!

...WHILE SOME ARE WAY OUT OF CHARACTER...

SOME OF THEM HAVE DIFFERENT ROLES...

WELL, HONESTLY, EVERYONE WAS ALREADY PRETTY CRAZY TO START WITH...

WHAT DO WE DO?

THE LONELY PUNCHLINE

BUT EVERYONE'S SILLINESS PRACTICALLY DEMANDS IT.

UGH. THIS SUCKS. I'VE NEVER BEEN GOOD AT POKING FUN.

NO, YOU'RE THE SHOCKING ONE!

THAT GAVE KYOKA A SHOCK!

JIRO USED TO BE THE QUIP-MASTER, BUT NOW SHE'S SOME KINDA LAID-BACK, CRUNCHY, AIRHEAD GAL?

TEE HEE HEE!

I'M GETTING LOST IN YOUR EYES, TODOROKI.

TH-THANKS.

Takes the card anyway

HIYA MIDORIYA. WANT THIS SUPER-RARE CARD FEATURING MY DEAR PAPA?

SPARKLE

WAIT, DID I JUST SET UP MY OWN PUNCHLINE?!

I'M A ONE-MAN SHOW!

SMAK

LIKE HELL I WANT THIS DUMB CARD!!

YIKES, MIDORIYA!

TOUGH PUNCHLINES

WHOA!

MINETA ACHIEVED ENLIGHTENMENT!

PLEASE GET STARTED ON YOUR TRAINING.

I DO NOT SEEK CONFLICT...

YOUR STRAP, YAOYOROZU!! FASTEN YOUR COSTUME'S STRAP!

BOING

I'LL EAT THESE LOSERS FOR BREAKFAST!!

YEAH, WELL SOMETHING ELSE IS ABOUT TO SLIP OUT INSTEAD!!

I'D JUST HAVE TO UNDO IT AGAIN WHEN I'M SLIPPING OUTTA THIS LATER.

BUT YOU GUYS USUALLY... ARGH!! S-SORRY!!

...

YOU'RE TERRIBLE.

HOW CRUDE, MIDORIYA.

USE THE FORCE, DEKU

H-HOW DOES THAT HELP, EXACTLY?

YOU'LL BE FINE! AFTER SPENDING SO MUCH TIME WITH THESE GUYS, I KNOW YOU CAN DO IT.

REALLY...?

NOPE. NO CLUE WHAT ANY OF THEM ARE THINKING.

BWAMP

AN EMOTIONAL SHOCK, THAT WHAMMIES SPACE-TIME ITSELF, HUH?

AN "OOPSIE"...?!

A BIG EMOTIONAL SHOCK...

DEKU!!

BOOBS.

BUT, HE MADE IT SOUND LIKE I'M SUPPOSED TO ENVISION HOW THEY USED TO BE.

I'VE SPENT SO MUCH TIME WITH THEM, SO I'LL SOMEHOW KNOW...

THREAD OF HOPE

GOTTA THINK UP A WAY TO GET BACK TO NORMAL...

ZUUUU

NOPE, NOPE, NOPE, NOPE, CAN'T TAKE THIS...

AHEM.

YES, I'M AWARE. I MADE A LITTLE OOPSIE WITH SPACE-TIME.

LISTEN! THIS IS A TOTAL MESS!

AN "OOPSIE"...?!

BAM

TIME

GOT A MOMENT, MIDORIYA?

IT'S YOU!!

YOU JUST NEED TO CAUSE AN EMOTIONAL SHOCK CRAZY ENOUGH TO WHAMMY SPACE-TIME ITSELF...

TIME

IT'S WITHIN THE MARGIN OF ERROR, SO THERE MAY BE A CHANCE TO FIX IT.

SORRY, I'M KIND OF...IN PRISON. CAN'T HELP YOU.

Sure thing!

Let's go take a dump!

TIME

HUH?! I NEED MORE DETAILS...

ACK!

NOO!!

118

THE BEGINNING OF THE BEGINNING

WITH THAT, OUR DIMENSION RETURNED TO NORMAL.

...

OH... SORRY!

HURRY UP, SLOWPOKE. WE'RE GONNA BE LATE.

FLAP

FLAP

ERO KING

MORE SKIN THAN EVER

THE TALE OF HOW WE BECAME GREAT HEROES.

BUT THE TRUE STORY STARTS HERE.

HUH?!

GASP

PAPA

PA...

PAPA.

FLAME KING

MORE SKIN THAN EVER

...BUT ALSO ENDLESS HOPE FOR THE FUTURE.

FWIP

A STORY FILLED WITH PLENTY OF CHALLENGES...

PLUS ULTRA!!

HUSH

GASP

119

THE FINAL VOLUME!! GREAT WORK!

Early on, I remember them saying this would only go to volume 3 or 4, so I'm so glad you got to do five whole books! But I'm even happier that this four-panel spin-off was a total delight all the way through! It's given me plenty of laughs, and I honestly wish I could keep reading! Here's hoping you get to draw more someday.

CAST OF CHARACTERS

NEDA:
AUTHOR OF SMASH!! UNEXPECTEDLY SERIOUS, DEEP DOWN.

HORIKOSHI:
AUTHOR OF MY HERO ACADEMIA. ONLY SERIOUS ABOUT MANGA.

SOME DOCTOR:
SOME DOCTOR. PROBABLY RIDICULOUSLY SERIOUS.

PHYSICAL THERAPIST:
A PHYSICAL THERAPIST. AT LEAST A LITTLE SERIOUS.

HORIKOSHI AND ME

FINAL CHAPTER: BOYS ON THE RUN

BADUM
BADUM

SO I JUST GOTTA WILL MYSELF TO HEAL IN UNDER A MONTH!!

LUCKILY, I ALREADY DREW FOUR CHAPTERS...

I CAN'T HOLD A PEN!!

KASHNK

LAST TIME, NEDA REALLY MESSED UP HIS HAND. HOW'S HE GONNA GET HIMSELF OUTTA THIS FIX?!

YEAH, SORRY. I SNEEZED, IT WENT FLYING OFF...

UNLIKELY, BUT OKAY!!

WHAT'S THAT? YOU REMOVED YOUR CAST?!

I'LL MAKE IT WORK!!

I JUST GOTTA HOLD IT LIKE THIS...

PINKY FINGER CAN'T MOVE AT ALL

IN THIS CAST, IT'S ONLY GOOD FOR PICKING BOOGERS!!

PLUS ULTRA !!

THIS HAND'S USELESS TO ME ANYWAY IF I FAIL NOW, SO HERE GOES...

KA

KRAK

Thank you, as always...

Here.

Todoroki's such a cutie.

Mt. Lady's just a metaphor for the modern working woman!

Okay. Sure...

JUST LIKE THAT, TWO YEARS PASSED...

Tsuyu, too.

Season 2 was so awesome.

Hang in there, Endeavor!!

PLEASE COMMENT:
WHAT DO YOU THINK OF SMASH!!..?

IT'S ENDING? OH NOOOOO!!

DON'T LET SMASH END

I KNEW ALL ALONG THE AUTHOR WAS CRAZY (IN A GOOD WAY)

DON'T LET IT END!!

THANK GOD IT'S OVER

THANK YOU

TODOROKI'S TOO GOOD AT BEING A PRINCE

...WHEN I HAD SUCH A HARD TIME DRAWING EVEN FIVE BOOKS...

IT'S A GOOD REMINDER OF HOW AMAZING HORIPI REALLY IS...

MANGA IS SERIOUSLY THE GREATEST THING EVER.

I'M SO GLAD I GOT TO DO THIS.

RUB RUB

URGH... THANK YOU. THIS POSITIVE ENERGY HELPED KEEP ME GOING ALL THIS TIME.

PRESS

...HORIPI KEPT RUNNING AHEAD, FULL THROTTLE.

WHILE I WAS BACK HERE, GOOFING AROUND...

...BUT WHAT DID I KNOW, REALLY?

I THOUGHT I WAS GETTING AN UP-CLOSE LOOK AT HIM...

...BUT I'LL RUN AS FAR AS I CAN GO TOO.

I MIGHT BE GETTING A DELAYED START...

WHAT A CLICHÉ!! THAT'S ALL YOU HAVE FOR ME?!

END

YUP. THE WORK SURE IS HARD, SO DO YOUR BEST.

THAT'S HOW I FEEL ABOUT YOU!! THAT'S WHAT THIS LITTLE SIDE COMIC WAS ALL ABOUT!!

HORIP!!

HORIP!...

SO, THANK YOU FOR READING *MY HERO ACADEMIA: SMASH!!* TO THE VERY END!!

THIS IS A BRUTAL INDUSTRY WITH PLENTY OF UPS AND DOWNS, SO THERE'S NO GUARANTEE WE'LL MEET AGAIN, BUT I DEFINITELY HOPE I GET TO DELIVER ANOTHER FUN MANGA TO YOU ALL, SOMEDAY!! THANK YOU FOR ALL YOUR SUPPORT. (BOW)

I MIGHT GET TO DRAW SOME SORT OF COMMEMORATIVE *SMASH!!* CONTENT FOR AN ANNIVERSARY OR SOMETHING, SO IF THAT HAPPENS, THINK BACK ON THE SERIES FONDLY.

FINALLY, THANK YOU TO HORIKOSHI, WHO ALWAYS PUTS UP WITH ALL OF MY NONSENSE. I'LL SPEND MY WHOLE LIFE TRYING TO REPAY YOU IN SOME SMALL WAY. ALSO, BIG THANKS TO MY EDITORS KOIKE AND FUJITA, WHO HELPED MAKE THIS SERIES POSSIBLE, AND MY FRIENDS AND FAMILY FOR THEIR SUPPORT. I'LL KEEP GIVING IT MY ALL!! IN SHORT, THANKS TO EVERYONE, FOR EVERYTHING. SEE YA!!

-HIROFUMI NEDA

THE STAFF

CONGRATS ON FINISHING THE SERIES! I CAN'T WAIT TO SEE WHAT YOU DO NEXT, NEDA!

SOME READERS MAY HAVE NOTICED THAT THE ART QUALITY SUDDENLY GOT A LOT BETTER, STARTING PARTWAY THROUGH VOLUME 4. THIS IS BECAUSE *SMASH!!* MANAGED TO HIRE AN ASSISTANT. HIS ART IS SO GOOD IT KIND OF SCARED ME, WHICH MAKES SENSE, BECAUSE HE'S ACTUALLY AN ARTIST IN ANOTHER INDUSTRY YOU ALL KNOW AND LOVE... THE THOUGHT OF ME GETTING TO HAVE AN ASSISTANT IS HONESTLY INSULTING TO THE ENTIRE SYSTEM, BUT HE HAD SOME FREE TIME AND OFFERED ME A FRIENDS AND FAMILY DISCOUNT. THANK YOU SO MUCH, YOSHIKAWA!! *SMASH!!* ONLY MANAGED TO GET COBBLED TOGETHER VIA A SERIES OF UNLIKELY MIRACLES.

MY HERO ACADEMIA: SMASH!! REJECTS

SOMETIMES THOSE WITHOUT A LEGAL WAY TO APPLY THEIR QUIRKS...

...FIND A WAY AROUND THE RULES.

MY HERO ACADEMIA VIGILANTES

In a superpowered society, there is nothing ordinary about evil anymore. Heroes, trained and licensed to protect and defend the public against supervillains, stand above all the rest. Not everyone can be a hero, however, and there are those who would use their powers to serve the people without legal sanction. But do they fight for justice in the shadows, or for reasons known only to themselves? What they fight for, they are called... Vigilantes.

VIGILANTE -BOKU NO HERO ACADEMIA ILLEGALS- © 2016 by Hideyuki Furuhashi, Betten Court, Kohei Horikoshi/SHUEISHA Inc.

MY HERO ACADEMIA

SCHOOL BRIEFS

ORIGINAL STORY BY KOHEI HORIKOSHI   **WRITTEN BY ANRI YOSHI**

Prose short stories featuring the everyday school lives of My Hero Academia's fan-favorite characters!

BOKU NO HERO ACADEMIA YUUEI HAKUSHO © 2016 by Kohei Horikoshi, Anri Yoshi/SHUEISHA Inc.

AKIRA TORIYAMA

DRAGON QUEST

ILLUSTRATIONS

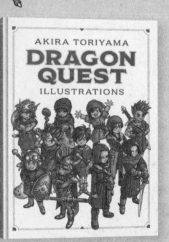

Akira Toriyama (*Dragon Ball*) brought the world of the renowned *Dragon Quest* video games to life through his creative, fun and inventive design work. Thirty years of genius are on display in this stunningly comprehensive hardcover collection of over 500 illustrations from the *Dragon Quest* video games. Includes fold-out poster of the *Dragon Quest* timeline.

A TORIYAMA DRAGON QUEST ILLUSTRATIONS © 2016 by BIRD STUDIO/SHUEISHA Inc.
GON QUEST SERIES: ©ARMOR PROJECT/BIRD STUDIO/SQUARE ENIX

VIZ

Dr. STONE

STORY BY
RIICHIRO INAGAKI

ART BY
BOICHI

One fateful day, all of humanity turned to stone. Many millenn
later, Taiju frees himself from petrification and finds hims
surrounded by statues. The situation looks grim—until he ru
into his science-loving friend Senku! Together they plan to resta
civilization with the power of science!

VIZ

DR. STONE © 2017 by Riichiro Inagaki, Boichi/SHUEISHA Inc.

THE ACTION-PACKED SUPERHERO COMEDY ABOUT ONE MAN'S AMBITION TO BE A HERO FOR FUN!

ONE-PUNCH MAN

STORY BY
ONE

ART BY
YUSUKE MURATA

Nothing about Saitama passes the eyeball test when it comes to superheroes, from his lifeless expression to his bald head to his unimpressive physique. However, this average-looking guy has a not-so-average problem—he just can't seem to find an opponent strong enough to take on!

Can he finally find an opponent who can go toe-to-toe with him and give his life some meaning? Or is he doomed to a life of superpowered boredom?

ONE-PUNCH MAN © 2012 by ONE, Yusuke Murata/SHUEISHA Inc.

www.viz.com

Ruby, Weiss, Blake
and Yang are
students at Beaco
Academy, learnin
to protect the wor
of Remnant from tl
fearsome Grimm

RWBY

MANGA BY **Shirow Miwa**
BASED ON THE ROOSTER TEETH SERIES
CREATED BY **Monty Oum**

RWBY © 2017 Rooster Teeth Productions, LLC
© 2015 by Shirow Miwa/SHUEISHA Inc.

viz.cor

YOU'RE READING THE WRONG WAY!!

My Hero Academia: Smash!! reads right to left, starting in the upper-right corner. Japanese is read right to left, meaning that action, sound effects and word balloon order are completely reversed from English order.